**This private & confidential workbook belongs to:**

_____

# JOURNEY TO RECOVERY

# A Return To The Self

## Donna Junker

**GreenWine Family Books™**
A division of GlobalEdAdvancePress

**JOURNEY TO RECOVERY: A Return to the Self**

Copyright © 2021 by Donna Junker

Library of Congress Control Number: 2021916000

Junker, Donna Kasik   1961 –

ISBN: 978-1-950839-15-5

Subjects:  1. Self-help – Twelve Step Programs;  2. Self-help – Motivational and Inspirational; 3. Religion – Christian Living, Personal Growth

Cover design by Global Graphics NYC

City of Publication: Nashville, TN

Printed in Australia, Brazil, France, Germany, Italy, Poland, Russia, Spain, UK, USA, and wherever there is an Espresso Book Machine

In addition to this workbook, the author's 2010 book, *Recovery: A Return to the Self,* ISBN 978-1-935434-51-1, is also available.

Books may be ordered at

www.gea-books.com/bookstore or

From the author at donnajunker@roadrunner.com

or any place good books are sold.

Published by

GreenWine Family Books

A division of

GlobalEdAdvance PRESS

# Contents

*What does it mean to "return to the self?"*
*Does that sound like a strange concept?*

# Preface

Journey to recovery and a return to the self simply involve recovering the person who God created us to be, who many of us have lost along life's journey for many reasons, such as: abandonment, betrayal, pain, addictions, loss, etc. God has a plan for all of our lives and, no matter what the circumstances were surrounding our births, God created each of us as a unique person who He wants in this life. We are all valuable to God, and He wants us to live up to our full potential.

I have noticed that people who believe in God, through Jesus Christ, and trust Him with their lives have a much higher success rate in their recovery than the people who do not place their lives and trust in God. This study will enable you to not only find your true self, and return to the self you may have lost (or may not have ever known, but who you long to be), but it will also lead you to a deep and personal encounter with God, through Jesus Christ, who can get you on the path to recovery. If you are not a "religious" person, hang in there with me. Each person will be given ample time to talk about their beliefs, in the hope that we will be open to learning about things that perhaps we have not heard before. We will all keep an open mind and respect one another. I write this because I care about people, about their recoveries, and because I strongly believe that faith in Jesus Christ can truly set us free; it did for me, so why would I not want to share that with others?

Recovery is not limited to addictions. Not all people suffer from addictions, but we all suffer from not always living as the people we want to be. We do not always do the things necessary to accomplish our dreams and goals, due to perhaps certain weaknesses and character defects that we ALL have and need to work on. Maybe you have tried recovery before and have failed; it's o.k. Let's try again, but this time, let's be completely open to God, rather than focusing only on ourselves. Maybe your dreams have been broken. I have a quote from the late British theologian, C.S. Lewis hanging in my house: *"The key to broken dreams is to dream again."* As we go through this journey to recovery, let's dream again…

This study can be done in any time frame that works for you or your group, and this workbook is not meant to be completed in any particular time frame or schedule. You can work through them at your own pace (or at the pace of the group if you are working with others). Take your time with this study, and allow yourself to be open to ideas and concepts that perhaps you are unfamiliar with, and be open to the working of God in your hearts and minds. We all have a story to tell. Our lives are a story that we will share as you feel comfortable. I will tell many stories of people I have met through my own journey to recovery, and I hope you will tell your stories as well on your own journey. Let's get started!

Answer a few basic questions to begin thinking about this concept of recovery and returning to self:

1.      Are you any different today from who you used to be? _____

_____

_____

2.      What has changed? _____

_____

_____

_____

_____

3.      What caused your change? _____

_____

_____

_____

_____

4.      Is there anything about yourself that you wish you could change?

_____

_____

_____

_____

5.      How can that change be made?_____

_____

_____

_____

_____

*"Forgetting what is behind and reaching forward to what is
ahead..."*   Philippians 3:13b

6.      What does that verse mean to you?_____

_____

_____

_____

_____

_____

The Bible has some very fundamental reasons as to why and how we
change, to the extent that we lose ourselves, and the Bible provides very real
examples of people in history who have also lost themselves through their
challenges and difficulties.  The Bible reveals how these same people found
themselves in real messes, but fortunately, the Bible also gives us the hope
and the direction to get us back on track and put us where we want to be in our
journey to recovery.  Even if you have never read the Bible or do not believe it,
it is the greatest piece of literature ever written, and can teach anyone much
about human nature and ourselves.  We all have spiritual longings because we

are spiritual creatures who sometimes <u>forget</u> who we are, where we are going, and where we belong in this life.  Together, we are going to try to answer those questions.  Let's start at the very beginning.

We are separated from God since, obviously, no one is perfect, while God is perfect.  Because of our separation from God, we have lost the person who God created us to be because sin entered the world.  Our thinking became distorted, our actions often became destructive, and some of our lives became a mess.  Fortunately, we have a God who can change all of that.  He can help us in our recovery.  He can return us to the self He originally created us to be.  He can bring us into a secure and loving relationship with Himself.  What does it mean to have a relationship with God? We will discuss this concept throughout this study.  Some people think that to grow in a relationship with God is "*to find our place, identity, and purpose*" (Benner p. 91).

First, we need to be very honest with ourselves and with one another.  We often deceive ourselves and others, trying to mask our pain or problems, or even normalize our messes.  Deception can creep in very easily and actually become a part of our lives.  Let's start with the Bible, which not only shows us who God is, but also uncovers human nature, with all of its problems and flaws.  The Bible thankfully, leads us to the hope that we find in God's unconditional love for us, and His acceptance of us, just as we are.

*Read Genesis chapter 3.*

▋ Did you notice any form of deception? Look at what Genesis 3:1 says, "*Did God actually say, 'You shall not eat of any tree in the garden'...*"? Now go back and read Genesis 2:16-17.  What type of deception was involved? _____

_____

▋ How easy is it to be deceived, or to hear only what we want to hear? Think of an example where you were deceived, or heard only what you wanted to hear, and twisted the meaning.  Did you try to justify your actions? _____ Has that played a role in any of the negative changes in your life? _____

_____

_____

▌ When you were deceived or tricked into doing something, did you blame others, especially if you were caught? _____

_____

The serpent tricked Eve, and she "ate" (did what she was told not to do). Eve said God told her she could not eat or touch the fruit in the middle of the garden, but is that what God said? Read Genesis 2:16-17 again.  Eve exaggerated and stretched the truth of what God told her and Adam, in order to get what she wanted.

▌ Can you think of an example when you exaggerated something to justify yourself or to get what you wanted at the moment? _____

_____

Eve ate the fruit that God told her not to eat, and then gave some to her husband Adam, who was right there all along and did not step in and stop her. *Read Genesis 3:6.* Adam knew they were told not to eat the fruit, yet he sat back and watched his wife disobey God.  The consequences were deadly.

▌ Have you ever passively sat back and watched a friend or spouse do things you knew were harmful, and did not step in?  Why?  Have you had friends/spouses do that to you, and refused to help?  What harm did that cause? What changed in your life as a result of that inaction? _____

_____

_____

*Read Genesis 3:8-12.* When Adam and Eve were "caught" by God, Adam first blamed God for even giving Eve to him, and then he blamed Eve, who in turn blamed Satan.

▌ In addition to perhaps blaming others for your problems, have you ever blamed God? _____

We need to take responsibility for our actions rather than blame other people and God. We often blame God for our own actions or inactions, or we blame Him for the works of the Enemy (Satan) who caused sickness, death, and evil. We are often mad at the wrong "person." In other words, people often blame God for the activity of Satan.

Knowing who we are is the first step in recovery, and in recovering who we were meant to be. You may have heard the saying, "Know thyself" which was said by the ancient Greek Philosopher Socrates, and his student Plato, and inscribed over the entrance of the Temple of Delphi in Greece. Socrates also taught that, "The unexamined life is not worth living." 2 Corinthians 13:5 says, "*Examine yourselves, to see whether you are in the faith. Test yourselves.*" Only when we know ourselves can we begin to see what is broken, what does not work, and then make the changes we want in our lives to live at peace.

### *This week, take some time and examine yourself:*

- Do you know who you are?
- Are you who you profess to be?
- Are you who you want to be?
- If you do claim to have a relationship with Jesus, are you indeed "living in the faith?"
- If you do not know Jesus, who or what is your Higher Power? How has that worked for you?
- Are you open to hearing about recovery through Jesus?
- Do you think recovery is possible? What would it take?

# NOTES

Jesus worked as a carpenter prior to beginning His earthly ministry.  I worked in the construction trades for over twenty-five years prior to becoming a chaplain.  I obviously do not know how construction workers did things two thousand years ago, but when I worked construction, the "bible" that we used was a set of blueprints that were necessary on each job site.  Without blueprints, workers have no idea what they are supposed to build, where anything goes, and what colors and finishes to use.

Life is like a job site; we need something to tell us how to live, what direction to go in, what is the right and wrong thing to do, etc.  We all need some type of instructions.  Life's blueprint is the Bible, and as some people say, the **B**asic **I**nstructions **B**efore **L**eaving **E**arth.  When I worked in the construction trades as a painter, I often worked on very large buildings in Chicago.  On one large job site in downtown Chicago, we could not find the blueprints, and knew we had to paint a room in one of the lower basements of this huge high-rise. Rather than continue to look for the prints, my foreman said he could figure out which room needed to be painted, and in our arrogance, we did not think we needed the blueprints; we thought we were smart enough without them.  We crawled (literally) into the room we thought needed to be painted since the doorway was only about 3' high, and began priming the walls, which were about twenty feet high.  Because the opening to the room was so small, we could not fit scaffolding or ladders into it, but had to stand on the floor and extend our rolling poles as far as they could go in order to reach the high walls.  If you have ever painted before, you know how difficult and heavy that is.  We were using block filler to prime the cinder block, which requires a very thick-napped roller, which is very heavy when soaked with block filler.  By the end of the day, we were both extremely tired and sore, and we dreaded the next day when we needed to put the finish coat over the block filler primer.  When we arrived at the job site that next day, we located the blueprints, only to discover that we had painted the wrong room! We went through all of that pain for nothing! When we walked over to the correct room, it had the standard 8' ceiling, with ladder access and was simple to prime and paint.  A lot of time, energy, and money were wasted because of our pride, because we did not take the time to find and read the blueprint.

▌ Have you ever wasted time, energy, and money because of pride?

▌ Have you ever in the past, or even today, think that you do not require the blueprint of life to help you navigate some very difficult and challenging areas in your life?

▌ If you do not read the Bible, what do you use for your moral compass? What do you rely upon to tell you right from wrong? What is your instruction manual for life? Do you even have one? How does it work out for you? Do we need one? Why or why not?

*We are here because we know we need a change*
*in the way we are currently living.  Let's go through*
*this journey together, and see who we can become,*
*and discover the beauty that awaits us...*

# Introduction

What types of people get trapped in some form of addiction, or a bad habit they cannot break, or a weakness they cannot overcome? ALL types! People who struggle with addictions are rich and poor, educated and uneducated, black and white, young and old.  Some of us who struggle with addictions have been told the lie that we are just bad people, or that we are weak.  It is easy then, to lose our feeling of self-worth, and maybe even stop trying to kick our habit and get our lives back on track.  The Bible, though, says we are all created In the image of God (Genesis 1:27), and therefore we all have inherent worth.  Remember the story of Adam and Eve, which is the basic story of human nature from the very beginning of time? Like them, who were both created perfectly, we mess up; it's not hard.  God created us perfectly, but He also gave us the freedom to make mistakes; we call it *free will.*  We can choose to live according to how God intended for us to live (in harmony and in peace), or we can choose to follow our own ways, which is often chaotic and ends up in disaster.  Do you ever feel restless? One of the great Church Fathers from North Africa, Saint Augustine once famously said, *"Our soul is restless until it finds rest in thee, O Lord; for you have made us for thyself"* (Benner, p. 95).  I hope we find rest in our hearts and minds in this study as we tap into the spiritual part of who we are.  We will look at parts of the Bible to help us because it is filled with great wisdom about the human condition and great advice for anyone.

The Bible is not a rule book filled with do's and don'ts, but is actually a common sense "blueprint" that shows us how to live a good and productive life.  When we become arrogant (that normal, human pride that we all have), we lose ourselves, and many of us became slaves to our weaknesses and addictions of various kinds.  Like my foreman and me in that large high-rise in Chicago, we got lost in that building and wasted time, energy, and money.  We thought we were doing the right thing, but were way off base! We totally messed up, wasted time, and lived through unnecessary pain.

The Bible says, *"For whatever overcomes a person, to that he is enslaved"* (2 Peter 2:19). We can be overcome by drugs, alcohol, sex, anger, bitterness, unforgiveness, or whatever that weakness is that we cannot overcome. We can find ourselves enslaved; however, we all inherently long to be free, right? Most of us do not even like to follow rules, yet we find ourselves slaves to our addictions, while longing to be free. No one ever woke up one day and said they wanted to be an addict, or a bitter person. Instead, addictions and character weaknesses (sin) seem to creep up on us; it can happen to the best of us. We lose ourselves. Are you the same person you were before you became addicted? I doubt it. You need to return to the self you were created to be, and become free. You can have a life-changing experience from bondage to freedom, which is what this journey to recovery is all about. The Bible addresses this problem that we all have, but thankfully, it also gives us a way out.

Romans chapter 6 says that if we give our lives over to Christ, He can set us free. When we finally give in and follow the teachings of the Bible and get baptized, we go through a type of symbolic death. Jesus was killed in a horrible way by crucifixion. When we get baptized, it symbolizes a death to our old self, and we rise to a new self that is finally free. Romans 6:6-11 says,

> *"We know that our old self was crucified with him in order that the body of sin might be brought to nothing, so that we would no longer be enslaved to sin. For one who has died has been set free from sin. Now if we have died with Christ, we believe that we will also live with him. We know that Christ, being raised from the dead, will never die again; death no longer has dominion over him. For the death he died he died to sin, once for all, but the life he lives he lives to God. So you also must consider yourselves dead to sin and alive to Christ Jesus."*

**It truly is possible to break those chains and be set free! Do you want to be free?** _____

This book is not just a self-help book, but instead, it is a guide to freedom and recovery through an encounter with God.  If you believe in God already, allow Him to take over and free you from your chains.  If you are unsure about God, or maybe do not believe in Him at all, I ask you to have an open mind; what will it hurt? Perhaps you have tried other recovery programs and stayed sober for a while, but fell right back into your old ways - a seemingly never ending battle.  The power of God is much greater than the power of ourselves, and He wants us to return to the self He created.  Some of us may have grown up in church, and know some of the stories of the Bible, but never really took it very seriously; after all, it's only a book.  That's like saying blueprints are only pieces of paper! However, we are lost without both.  We need the basic Truth and understanding of Scripture.  We need to be the people we know we can be.  We need a return to the self.

During this study, we will look at the Bible as our blueprint for life.  In the Old Testament book of Joshua, and the New Testament book of Hebrews, God promised never to leave us or forsake us (Joshua 1:5 & Hebrews 13:5).  Many of us have been abandoned or betrayed by people in our lives, but that will never happen with God; He remains with us through our struggles.  When Jesus came to earth, He said that He, *"Came that they may have life and have it abundantly"* (John 10:10).  An abundant life is a life of peace and freedom, which recovery will give us.  We do not need to live in chaos, confusion, brokenness, and pain, unable to conquer our addictions and demons.  We have a blueprint for our lives (the Bible) that will help us navigate those dark hallways and get us to where we want to be, and bring us into the light.  We do not need to stumble around aimlessly, trying to figure out who we are and what is our lives' purpose.  When we ignore God, when we do not read His Word and live in His Truth, we distance ourselves from God, and we lose ourselves.

*"Imagine yourself as a living house.  God comes in to rebuild that house.  At first, perhaps, you can understand what He is doing.  He is getting the drains right and stopping the leaks in the roof and so on; you knew that those jobs needed doing and so you are not surprised.  But presently He starts knocking the house about in a way that hurts abominably and does not seem to make any sense. What on earth is He up to? The explanation is that He is building quite a different house from the one you thought of – throwing out a new wing here, putting on an extra floor there, running up towers, making courtyards.  You thought you were being made into a decent little cottage: but He is building a palace.  He intends to come and live in it Himself."* – C.S. Lewis

# Introduction to the Twelve Steps

Many of you may be familiar with the Twelve Step of Alcoholics Anonymous; I used those steps as a chaplain when I facilitated spirituality groups in various hospitals where I worked.  Through those spirituality groups that I facilitated, the responses I received, and the many conversations I had with patients, I developed my own Twelve Steps, which had more of a biblical component, which are the steps we will go through on this journey to recovery. Each week we will go into detail on each step, but here is an overview to give you an idea of the direction we will take on our journey to recovery.

### The Twelve Steps:

1. Admit that at times, we all pretend and are hypocritical.
2. Acknowledge that we are lost.
3. Discover God through Jesus Christ.
4. Begin to develop a Christ-centered world view.
5. Learn to see God in daily life.
6. Deny yourself for the sake of loving others.
7. Allow Jesus to be more, and yourself to be less.
8. Learn to love, help, and live selflessly.
9. Understand your will as it conflicts with God's will.
10. Learn to trust, love, and obey God completely.
11. Understand safety as found in Scripture and in the center of God's will.
12. Recover yourself through Scripture.

If you are not a Christian, these twelve steps may sound foreign to you, but I believe you will still find strength and value as we go through them.  If you are already a Christian, we will learn to apply our faith in a deeper way and see how it will enable us to find complete recovery and a new life through a deeper understanding of the Bible and God.  Let's begin with a few ideas before looking in depth at our Twelve Steps.

## The Deceptions in Life

Most of us (perhaps all of us, to varying degrees), want God on our own terms.  We want God to be whoever we create Him to be, the God of our understanding, as AA states.  We want God to give in to our desires and plans, instead of asking God what He wants for us.  In a sense, we want God to give in to us, rather than us giving up everything for Him.  If we can create our own God, then is He still God? I had a pastor friend years ago who said if we could understand God, He would cease to be God, but would just be one of us.  How then do we know who God is or what He is like? For Christians, it is through the Bible.  There is a saying that desperate people do desperate things.  Do you agree? Many desperate people attend AA meetings, which have helped many, many people in their recovery.  As in all good things however, deceptions can creep in, and a desperate alcoholic can be an easy target.  Step Three of the Twelve Steps says that we "Made a decision to turn our lives over to the care of God as we understood Him" (Twelve Steps, p. 34).  This is a wonderful step, especially with people who have a "problem" with God, who want nothing to do with Him, who grew up in a church that was over-bearing or caused hurt.  I think however, there is a danger in Step Three since *we* create God, instead of God being the Creator; He then ceases to be God.

Years ago, when I was a chaplain at a hospital in West Virginia, one woman told me her higher power was a rock, which was her god, "as she understood him." As expected, her higher power did not work out very well, and she continued to fail in her recovery.  She invented her own god, rather than discovering who the real God is, who could have indeed helped her to recover from her addiction.  How do we discover God? Is that even possible? Yes.  The Bible is where God reveals Himself and shows us who He is: a God of love, of mercy, of forgiveness, of power.  In Exodus 34:6, God said He is *"merciful and gracious, slow to anger, and abounding in steadfast love and faithfulness,"* and in

Numbers 14:18, God said once again that He is *"slow to anger, and abounding in steadfast love, forgiving iniquity and transgressions."* God is filled with more love and forgiveness than any person we can ever imagine. We simply cannot create a better God than the one we already have.

Many people in AA or NA claim to know things *about* God, but many do not actually *know* God, or the power He possesses to help them overcome their addictions or weaknesses. I had a friend who found sobriety through AA, but he told me that when he got to step Three, he did not know much about God, even though he grew up in church and knew the basics. He told me something though that I found astonishing; he said, "If your god doesn't work for you, fire him and find a new one!" Basically, you do whatever you need to do to stay sober, including creating a Creator to fit your whims. A God I can create is not very powerful...

We have already discussed how we can be deceived when we learned about Eve (in the book of Genesis) and how she was deceived by Satan when he twisted God's words. Any of us, even the most intelligent of us, can be deceived. Probably most of us would like a god who goes along with whatever we want to do, rather than a God who gives us His guidelines for our own good. We fall back into our adolescence when we did not want to follow our parent's rules. It is only after we grew up and became adults that we realized our parents had rules and curfews for our safety because they loved us; God is the same way. He has rules, such as the Ten Commandments, that He put in place for our own good. We need to take God on His terms, and not try to get Him to bend to ours (as if that were even possible!) If we follow the basic instructions of the Bible, we will not wander around lost, making things up as we go along, and creating our own false gods. Galatians 6:7, 9, &10 says, *"Do not be deceived; God is not mocked, for whatever one sows, that he will also reap...And let us not grow weary in doing good, for in due season we will reap, if we do not give up. So then, as we have opportunity, let us do good to everyone, and especially to those who are of the household of faith."* God is truly love.

*Do you think it is possible not to be loved by God? Who is God (or your higher power) and can He actually help you in recovery?* _____

_____

_____

_____

## Defining the Terms

I once asked a musician friend of mine about his Christian faith, how it applied to his life, and how often he read the Bible in order to understand just what the Christian faith actually is; he responded in a very unusual way. He said, "My faith is like a piece of music; when you don't have the sheet music in front of you, and you're not sure which exact notes to sing, you just listen, and you sing in the spirit of the music. You don't have to have it exact and perfect. I live in the spirit of my faith, and just do the best I can." I was shocked. If the sheet music is available, and you are perhaps simply too lazy to get it and learn the music, there is no excuse. If others were trying to sing along with him, and he basically just went with the flow, making things up as he went along, he would trip others up and cause them to stumble. When we have the Bible available to us, why make things up as we go along, and possibly cause not just ourselves to stumble in our recovery, but also those around us? When we have the answers available to us, why not search them out and get it right? Following the principles in the Bible and allowing the love and power of God to work through us is what will help us get recovery right, especially if we have tried and failed in the past. First, though, we need to define some basic principles.

So what is this Christian faith I keep mentioning? It is a faith that believes that there is a God, not just a higher power out there, but a God who is intimately involved in each of our lives, who created all of us in His image, and who loves us more than we can ever imagine. The Christian faith is defined in the Bible, which tells us who God is, what He is like, and what He desires for us – an abundant, peaceful, and sober life with meaning and purpose. We do not have to guess what the words are, singing off key and confusing everyone around us, but we can know for certain how to live. My musician friend's faith is as confusing to me as wandering around a huge sky scraper, guessing what room to paint! We unknowingly destroy ourselves and those around us through our lack of knowledge and laziness, when there is no need to create this chaos and unnecessary pain.

The Bible often compares human beings to sheep. Unfortunately, sheep are not the smartest animals, and they are helpless and vulnerable to attack without a shepherd to care for them. Sheep do not see very well; they can easily fall into a ditch of which they are unable to climb out of, and would lie there until they died of starvation, dehydration, or were attacked by another animal such as a wolf. Sheep have a tendency to wander off and get lost; they need a shepherd to guide them. Many of us know the familiar 23rd Psalm:

*"The Lord is my shepherd; I shall not want.*
*He makes me lie down in green pastures.*
*He leads me besides still waters;*
*He restores my soul.*
*He leads me in paths of righteousness*
*For His name's sake.*
*Even though I walk through the valley of the shadow of death,*
*I will fear no evil,*
*For you are with me;*
*Your rod and your staff, they comfort me.*
*You prepare a table before me*
*In the presence of my enemies;*
*You anoint my head with oil;*
*My cup overflows.*
*Surely goodness and mercy*
*Shall follow me all the days of my life*
*And I shall dwell in the house of the Lord,*
*Forever."*

Does that not sound like a kind, caring, and loving shepherd?  That is who God is.  He wants to guide us and keep us from getting lost and hurt.  He wants to protect us.  He wants to give us good things.  Jesus called Himself the Good Shepherd, who walks with his sheep and stays with them at all times, keeping them safe.  Shepherds use their rod and staff to bring sheep back who are wandering off and getting into trouble.  How many times have we wandered off? Shepherds love, guide, protect, and care for their sheep.  People need protection, and Jesus said He is the one who will protect us from harm if we simply follow Him.  Just as guardrails on highways or crossing gates at train tracks are there for our protection, God's "rules" for life protect us too.  The Good Shepherd does not want any of His sheep to perish.

Human nature is rebellious and generally does not like to follow rules.  People who do not understand the Christian faith think the Bible is nothing but a set of rules we are supposed to follow, which are too hard and take all the fun of life away; that is absolutely not true.  Recovering ourselves to who God created us to be does in a way have "rules" to follow, but what in life that is worthwhile does not? There are "rules" to loving relationships such as marriage.  What if one spouse told the other that they had no obligations or commitments to them? What if one spouse thought there was no need for honesty or faithfulness, or even kindness?  What if spouses did not think there was any "rule" about love and respect for the other?  What relationship exists without some parameters or rules, if you will? These so called "rules" are for the mutual benefit and happiness of the people involved, right? The Bible has two basic rules: *Love God and love others as you love yourself* (Matthew 22:37-39).  If you can follow those two "rules," you are on the right track.

"Rules" can also be life-saving.  When I was 39 years old, I took sky-diving lessons.  The first time anyone jumps out of a perfectly good airplane, there are some basic rules they must follow.  One rule is to make sure you have a parachute, plus a backup chute, and your altimeter (which is a devise sky diver's wear on their wrists to keep track of their height).  One generally jumps out of the plane at 13,500 feet, and free-falls at 120 miles per hour until he/she reaches

5,500 feet, when it is time to pull the rip cord that releases the parachute. The altimeter is like the sky-diver's bible, that, when followed correctly, leads one to safety. Once the chute is pulled and the diver slows down, the ride to the ground is beautiful. Living a clean and sober life, following the principles of loving God and your neighbor as yourself, is also a beautiful life, and one where you are not looking over your shoulder or worried about things such as the law, jail, or overdosing. Sobriety allows us to slow down and enjoy the ride of life.

Temptations accompany recovery. Often, the most worthwhile things in life require the most work. In the New Testament book of Luke chapter 4, Jesus Himself was tempted. He had been fasting for many days and was hungry, and Satan came along and said, "*If you are the Son of God, command this stone to become bread*" (Luke 4:3). When we are the most vulnerable, is when we are the most tempted. Jesus was tempted two more times, but He never gave in to the temptation. The Bible says that there is no temptation that we cannot overcome with the help of God (1 Corinthians 10:13). We can stay clean and sober, even when tempted, because God has the power to help us if we ask Him. Jesus understood temptation, because He was also tempted when He was at His weakest.

*Think about your recovery: is this the first time you are in recovery? Have you tried before and the temptations became too strong? What will you do this time to resist temptation and remain clean and sober, or focused on your goals, strengthening your weaknesses, and pursuing right living?* __

_____

_____

_____

_____

## The Grace of God

All of us want to be happy, we want to be safe, and we want to be loved. God's grace can provide all of these things in our lives. Many of us do not understand grace because we have never experienced grace, nor do we live in grace ourselves.  What is grace? It is undeserved help, undeserved forgiveness, and undeserved love.  We do not deserve these things from God, but He freely gives them anyway.  What about our actions towards other people? If someone has hurt us, can we still love them? Can we forgive them? Would we ever help them? Doing those things implies that we love our neighbor as ourselves, right? When Jesus was literally being nailed to the Cross by people who hated Him and made fun of Him, He actually said, *"Father forgive them, for they know not what they do"* (Luke 23:34).  Can you even begin to imagine love and forgiveness to that extent?

God's grace though, sometimes includes discipline.  If you are a parent and your child is doing something wrong, even dangerous, like running out into the street, don't you discipline with maybe a spanking or a grounding? Why? Is it because you hate your child and are a mean parent, or because you love your child and want to ensure their safety? God is the same way.  God sets His "rules" or boundaries for us for our own good, for our safety and protection, and because He loves us.  We find God's "rules" in the Bible.

I have mentioned the Bible many times now; what exactly is it? The Bible is considered the greatest piece of literature ever written.  It has numerous authors and was written over 1500 years.  It is filled with stories, history, poetry, drama, and letters.  If you are new to the Bible, I suggest beginning with the New Testament, which begins with Matthew, and read the four gospels: Matthew, Mark, Luke, and John, and then continue to the end.  The Bible beautifully paints a description of what God is like through the life-stories of many people in this Book, and we cannot help but fall in love with Jesus because of His great love for people.  Throughout the Bible, we read about failure after failure of even the greatest of people who God continued to love and used in powerful ways.  God still loves us through our failures too, and can use us in this life.  Each time the great people of the Bible did something stupid and fell, when they asked for forgiveness and acknowledged their messes, God forgave them, loved them, and restored them to their purposes in life.  The Bible is basically a book about the amazing love and grace of God, displayed over and over, despite human failure that is committed over and over.

Many new readers of the Bible do not understand the Old Testament, so for now, we will focus on the New Testament. I want to say just a few words about the Old Testament though before we move on. It is composed of 39 books, sectioned into three basic divisions: The Law, the Prophets, and the Writings, which includes Wisdom literature. The very first book of the Old Testament is Genesis, where Adam and Eve messed up right away, yet God continued to love them. God forgave them, and He offered His grace. God loves His people so much that He refuses to let them go. Basically, the Old Testament is about how people messed up, and how God extended His grace. It is never too late to obtain God's blessings and grace, no matter what we have done in the past.

The New Testament contains 27 books, arranged in four sections: The Gospels, the Acts of the Apostles, the Letters, and the Apocalypse. The New Testament tells us about the life of Jesus and the beginning of the Christian Church, while it instructs us in how to live well. The word "*gospel*" literally means "good news," which is what the Bible gives us. We have the good news that no matter how bad we have been, no matter how many times we have failed, we are still loved by God, and He wants to help us in our recovery. The very first church, as recorded in the book of Acts, had problems (just as churches today have problems). I once heard someone say that you will never find a perfect church, because _you_ (any of us) will be in it. We are all flawed, imperfect, broken people who God wants to restore. God never intended for us to wander around like lost sheep, exposed to dangers, or like lost painters in a high-rise without a blueprint, or like musicians who cannot read music or fail to obtain it. God loves us far too much to leave us to ourselves. We will use the Bible as our blueprint as we journey through the twelve steps, learn from one another, and hopefully along the way, find a loving God who will recover the person we lost along life's bumpy roads.

*Have you ever read the Bible? Are you open to learning anything from it?*
*Do you think it can help you in your recovery?*

_____

_____

_____

_____

# Step One:

## Admit That At Times, We All Pretend
## And Are Hypocritical

Some of us remember Bob Dylan's song, "*Blowin' in the Wind*" released back in 1963. A line from that very famous song says, "*How many roads must a man walk down, before you can call him a man?*" Years ago, I saw a bumper sticker that read, "*How many roads must a man walk down before he admits he is lost*?" We can all get lost in life by walking down the wrong roads, and we lose our very selves in the process. When we do not have our roadmap or our blueprint (the Bible), we usually mess up quite a bit down the roads of life, and we need to admit we are lost; that is where we need to begin. Most of us do not want to admit that we are lost though, so we keep making the same mistakes and we get more and more lost. Some of us may have heard the "definition" of insanity: we keep doing the same things but expect different results! Maybe we pretend everything is fine in front of our family and friends, even when we know things are not fine, and we act like a hypocrite. We need a spiritual recovery, since as humans we are both physical beings with bodies, and spiritual beings with souls. We need to stop pretending and get on the right path.

In the Old Testament, we find the story of Moses leading the Israelites out of slavery in Egypt, into the Promised Land that God had provided for them to live in and to be free. They traveled for forty years to reach the Promised Land, though in actuality, the journey should have taken just a little more than a week! The Israelites continually complained and disobeyed God's commands (given through Moses), and they wandered around for years. Perhaps you have been wandering around lost in the wilderness of life, perhaps of your own making, or from tragedies that have happened to you; either way, we can get back on the right path and begin to shorten our difficult journeys. Throughout the Israelites' journey in the wilderness, God promised to be with them, just as he does for us today; we are never on our own.  Let's begin with some of our own wilderness wanderings:

▌ What do you fill your life with in order to escape pain or boredom? _____

_____

_____

▌ Do you have any regrets? _____What are they? _____

_____

▌ Do you think perhaps you will wait until you are old to start thinking about Jesus, since you believe following Him will take away your fun?

_____

*Read Luke 12:35-48*

▌ Does following God really take away our fun?

_____

▌ How does God "speak" to us? _____

_____

Many of us wrestle with pride; we think we are pretty smart.  King Solomon was considered the wisest man who ever lived, at least at that time (900s B.C.) I have heard many addicts say they are too smart to overdose, and they know what they are doing; that is pride.  Many of those same people are now dead – from an overdose.  We do sometimes pretend to be people we are not; we can be quite hypocritical.  It is foolish to think more of ourselves than we actually are, and not acknowledge that we can make bad choices, and that, yes, we can make fatal choices.  To wait until we are old to think about changing, or to think about "religion" or God is foolish since none of us are guaranteed old age and long lives.  How many people do you know who died young? Probably quite a few.

Let's read a parable from the New Testament:

*"Stay dressed and ready for action and keep your lamps burning, and be like men who are waiting for their master to come home*

*from the wedding feast, so that they may open the door to him at once when he comes and knocks. Blessed are those servants whom the master finds awake when he comes. Truly, I say to you, he will dress himself for service and have them recline at table, and he will come and serve them. If he comes during the second watch, or in the third, and finds them awake, blessed are those servants! But know this, that if the master of the house had known at what hour the thief was coming, he would not have let his house be broken into. You must also be ready, for the Son of Man is coming at an hour you do not expect…Who then is the faithful and wise manager whom his master will set over his household, to give them their portion of food at the proper time? Blessed is that servant whom his master will find so doing when he comes. Truly, I say to you, he will set him over all his possessions. But if the servant says to himself, 'My master is delayed in coming' and he begins to beat the male and female servants, and to eat and drink and get drunk, the master of that servant will come on a day he does not expect him and at an hour that he does not know, and will cut him in pieces and put him with the unfaithful. And that servant who knew his master's will but did not get ready or act according to his will, will receive a severe beating"* (Luke 12:35-39 & 42-48).

None of us have any idea when the world will end or when we are going to die. What is the above parable saying? _____

_____

_____

_____

▌ How many people do you know who died unexpectedly, maybe from an auto accident or an overdose? _____

▌ Are you fooling yourself into thinking that could never happen to you? _____ What comes next, after this life? _____

_____

_____

▌ Are you ready?_____ If not, what do you need to do? _____

_____

▮ What needs to take place in your life? _____

_____

_____

▮ What are the consequences of our actions? _____

_____

_____

▮ Do you ever pretend there are no consequences? _____

_____

In the Old Testament, there is a "wisdom" book entitled, Ecclesiastes. Many scholars believe Ecclesiastes was written by King Solomon, one of the wisest men to have ever lived. In his later years, he contemplated his life and life in general. Despite being wise, Solomon walked down quite a few roads, and admitted later that he got lost along the way. He tried to find meaning and pleasure in sex, alcohol, money, and power, but in the end, he said, "*I have seen everything that is done under the sun, and behold, all is vanity, and striving after wind*" (Ecclesiastes 1:14). Why would he say that? Solomon lost himself spiritually, doing his own thing apart from the Law of God, which at that time, was the first five books of the Bible in the Old Testament. The full Bible was not yet written. We can learn from the mistakes of others by reading the Bible, especially since it is full of stories of people who lost themselves by choosing roads that led to their ultimate destruction. Solomon's father was King David, who taught his son to follow the commands of God, including, "*You shall have no other gods before me*" (Exodus 20:3). A god is anything we put before all else in our life.

▮ What might another "god" be for us?

_____

_____

▮ Have you ever thought that you might be your own god? _____
How? _____

▮ Have you ever known that something was wrong, against all that you learned as a child, and against the truth of the Bible, but did it anyway?

_____ If so, you became your own god.  Is that hypocritical?  ___

_____

When we move away from the wisdom of the Bible and live in ways contrary to what God intends, the loss of self begins...

## Money

Solomon pursued wealth, which was one of his "gods." He wrote, *"I made great works.  I built houses and planted vineyards for myself. I made myself gardens and parks, and planted in them all kinds of fruit trees.  I made myself pools from which to water the forest of growing trees.  I bought male and female slaves, and had slaves who were born in my house.  I had also great possessions of herds and flocks, more than any who had been before me in Jerusalem. I also gathered for myself silver and gold and the treasure of kings and provinces."* (Ecclesiastes 2:4-8a).  Despite his wealth, Solomon still concluded that *"all is vanity and a chasing after the wind."* He wrote, *"What has a man from all the toil and striving of heart with which he toils beneath the sun?  For all this days are full of sorrow, and his work is a vexation.  Even in the night his heart does not rest.  This also is vanity"* (Ecclesiastes 2:22-23).  King Solomon concluded, *"He who loves money will not be satisfied with money, nor he who loves wealth with his income; this also is vanity"* (Ecclesiastes 5:10).  Money can become our god, and the Bible warns, *"For the love of money is a root of all kinds of evils.  It is through this craving that some have wandered away from the faith and pierced themselves with many pains"* (1 Timothy 6:10).

■ Have you ever experienced pain in trying to get money in ways other than working for it, or that you wanted for the wrong purposes?

_____

_____

_____

■ If so, was money your god, or was your god the thing(s) you wanted to purchase with that money? _____

_____

Money in and of itself is not evil, but the love of money often leads us to do many stupid things! It is when we make money our god that the evil creeps in. Also, evil often creeps in with what you spend that money on!

## Pleasure

King Solomon also desired to live for pleasure, as he wrote, "*I searched with my heart how to cheer my body with wine… and how to lay hold of folly, till I might see what was good for the children of man to do under heaven during the few days of their life… I also gathered for myself silver and gold and the treasures of kings and provinces. I got singers, both men and women, and many concubines, the delight of the sons of man*" (Ecclesiastes 2:3&8). He went on to say, "*And whatever my eyes desired I did not keep from them. I kept my heart from no pleasure, for my heart found pleasure in all my toil, and this was my reward for my toil. Then I considered all that my hands had done and the toil I had expended in doing it, and behold, all was vanity and a striving after the wind, and there was nothing to be gained under the sun*" (Ecclesiastes 2:10-11).

Our normal, human desires can become addictive and out of control. Solomon mentioned his over-indulgence in both women (sex) and wine. Both "pleasures" can get out of control.

- Is there anything "pleasurable" that you find yourself addicted to? (Sex, drugs, alcohol, etc.) _____
- Do you need help overcoming your addiction? _____
- What steps do you need to take to end your addiction(s)? _____

_____

_____

_____

- Do you ever pretend your addiction is not a problem? _____

Pleasure and sensuality can easily become our gods and get placed before the commands of God. For example, God created sex primarily for procreation, but also for pleasure, though He placed protective boundaries around it for our physical, emotional, and spiritual health. Genesis 1:27-28 says,

*"So God created man in his own image, in the image of God he created him; male and female he created them. And God blessed them. And God said to them, 'Be fruitful and multiply, and fill the earth and subdue it."* One of the first "commands" God gave to people was to have sex, but He set up parameters and protections for us for our own well-being.

British theologian C.S. Lewis wrote in his book, *Christian Behavior*, *"There's a story about a schoolboy who was asked what he thought God was like. He replied that, as far as he could make out, God was, 'The sort of person who is always snooping around to see if anyone is enjoying himself and then trying to stop it.'"* (Lewis, p. 1).

▮ What do you think of the above quote by C.S. Lewis? _____

_____

_____

▮ What do you think are the parameters God set up around sex for our protections? _____

_____

_____

▮ Do you live within those parameters? _____ Why or why not?

_____

_____

_____

▮ What are some of the negative consequences we can face when we live outside of God's plan for sexuality? _____

_____

_____

▮ Why do you think God has a "narrow" view of sexuality? _____

_____

_____

(Think about unplanned pregnancies, STD's, pain in breakups / divorce, raising children as a single parent, etc.).

▌ Have you ever thought that maybe the "rules" we learned as children are for our own good? _____

▌ Can you think of examples of how following the "rules" and having boundaries in place are for our own good and protections? _____

_____

_____

_____

(Consider rules of the road: solid yellow lines, barriers along roads, speed limits, etc.).

The Bible describes the down-fall of the great King Solomon in 1 Kings 11, which began when he wandered away from the self God had originally created him to be, and lived in ways contrary to what he knew was right. Solomon suffered the consequences for his wrong actions/addictions, and followed other "gods" besides the true God. *"And the Lord was angry with Solomon, because his heart had turned away from the Lord, the God of Israel, who had appeared to him twice, and had commanded him concerning this thing, that he should not go after other gods. But he did not keep what the Lord commanded. Therefore the Lord said to Solomon, 'Since this has been your practice and you have not kept my covenant and my statutes that I have commanded you, I will surely tear the kingdom from you and give it to your servant. Yet for the sake of David your father I will not do it in your days, but I will tear it out of the hand of your son"* (1 Kings 11:9-12).

▌ Has anything of value been torn away from you as a result of your addictions or hypocrisy, pretending everything was fine, when it was not fine at all? _____

_____

_____

*"The Lord opens the eyes of the blind."*
(Psalm 146:8)

# Step Two:

## Acknowledge That We Are Lost

As part of my own journey, I went to Calcutta, India to work at Mother Teresa's home for the dying. Mother Teresa has always been someone I so greatly admired, so I contacted her Missionaries of Charity and organized my trip. (Unfortunately, I never did get to meet Mother Teresa because she had already died). I was a hospice chaplain at the time, and I thought of her home for the dying as the ultimate hospice. What a wonderful opportunity to learn! Calcutta is a very loud, dirty, poverty-stricken, smelly city with narrow streets that all looked the same to me. Every Monday, Wednesday, and Friday at 3:00, volunteers from all over the world register with the Missionaries of Charity for their work assignment. I chose to work at Kalighad, the original site that Mother Teresa began years ago, where the sick and dying homeless people are taken in from off of the street and given a clean cot inside the building, food and drink, and are bathed and cared for so they do not have to die alone on the streets. Work would begin the following morning.

I enjoyed the difficult work at Kalighad, and met many people from all over the world; it was indeed very interesting. Lisa was an American woman who was also traveling alone to work in Calcutta, and we became friends while we were in India. It was dark that first evening when we finished our work, and we were both uncertain how to get back to our respective hotels; I only knew the basic direction of how to get there (but no details). Lisa and I were staying in different places, but she had heard of the hotel where I was staying and wanted to see it. A rickshaw driver motioned to us for a ride, so we climbed in for what we assumed would be a safe ride back. I told our driver to take us to the Fairlawn Hotel on Sudder Street; he nodded and immediately went in the wrong direction! I tapped him on the back and said, "The Fairlawn Hotel…you are going in the wrong direction." He nodded, turned around, and began to jog. I knew we had at least a mile or more to go, but after just a few blocks he stopped and motioned for us to get out. It was dark, and I told him no, we would not get out since we were not yet at the hotel. Lisa and I did not budge. The driver appeared frustrated, but continued. We realized our rickshaw driver might not have spoken English, and actually had no idea where he was going. He stopped again and motioned for us to get out, and once again we refused. The dark, narrow streets did not look familiar at all, so I knew we were lost. We proceeded to go down some other dark, narrow streets, and I had no idea where we were. Our driver may have been lost and seemed to have no idea where the Fairlawn Hotel was either. Lisa and I knew we were lost, and were a little frightened. We did not know how to get to the hotel. Several more times our driver motioned for us to get out, but we refused since we had no idea where we were.

▮ Have you ever had someone take you down the dark, narrow streets of life, lost himself, and also got you lost in the process? _____

▮ Did you go along for the ride? _____

▮ Did you venture out in the middle of the darkness and confusion, knowing you were not in a good and safe place? _____

▮ What happened after that? _____

_____

_____

I finally saw a building that had the words "Sudder Street" written on it, so we got out, paid his wage, and finally headed in the right direction. I thought of Jeremiah 50:6, which says, "*My people have been lost sheep. Their shepherds have led them astray.*" Without the words "Sudder Street" on that building, I would not have been able to locate my hotel. Without the Truth in the words of Scripture, our blueprint, we also get lost and cannot find our way as we ride through the darkened streets of our lives. With just one wrong turn, we can easily fumble around in the darkness, and in fear, we try to find our way back home, but are uncertain how to get there.

▌ Have you ever felt lost in a sense, and unsure how to get where you wanted to be? _____

▌ How did you find your way "home," or are you still wandering around lost? _____

_____

_____

▌ What does it take to get back on track and know where we are going?

_____

_____

_____

On a day off of work, I decided to walk the streets of Calcutta to familiarize myself with them (especially after getting lost that night!) and to fully experience this strange city. The streets were dirty and narrow, filled with outdoor shops with curtains where many people lived, which they just rolled up in the morning to begin their days. All of the streets looked the same to me as I wound my way through the very crowded streets. I was distracted looking at the various shops, the meat carcasses hanging in the hot sun with flies all around them, and into the faces of these very different people. Everyone had empty, blank stares to me, and their faces seemed sad, desperate, hungry, and lonely. I looked into so many people's eyes, and saw nothing. Goats and cows walked the streets, rummaging through the garbage for food, fighting the children for a scrap. Animals and people alike relieved themselves on the streets, which of course smelled. I began to have that sinking feeling that once again, I was lost. I had no idea where I was or how to get back to my hotel. I was scared, and thought if I just looked confident and pretended to know where I was, no one would bother me, I would be safe, and eventually find my way to the hotel. Fortunately, I found some policemen and asked them for directions to my hotel. Without those men, I would have continued wandering around lost.

▌ Have you ever pretended everything was o.k. and that you knew what you were doing, when all along you knew you were lost and in an unsafe place in your life? _____

_____

∎ Do you think it is a good thing to ask for help? _____ Why or why
not? _____

_____

∎ Do you think people need one another? _____

∎ How does being in community, or having an accountability partner
(sponsor) help keep us from getting lost? _____

_____

_____

When I worked as a hospice chaplain in the Appalachian Mountains,
in Eastern Kentucky, I met many very interesting people. One man I met was
named Arnold, who was dying of cancer. Arnold and his wife lived in a small,
run-down wooden shack in the middle of nowhere, and I visited them often. One
day I asked if they wanted the Lord's Supper, and Arnold said something that
surprised me. He said he probably should not because he had "fallen away
from the Lord and not lived as he should." I respected Arnold for his honesty
in acknowledging that he was lost, but I also reminded him of God's love and
forgiveness towards us.

∎ Have you ever felt beyond God's love for something(s) you did in your
life? _____

∎ Do you think it is possible for God not to love or forgive us?
_____ Why or why not? _____

_____

∎ Do you truly believe God passionately loves you and wants to be in your
life? _____ Why or why not? _____

_____

*"And I said: 'Woe is me! For I am lost; for I am a man of unclean lips...'"*

(Isaiah 6:5)

# Step Three:

## Discover God Through Jesus Christ

Early on in my trip to India, I decided to go and see the famous Hindu temple called Kalighat, named after one of their many gods. My taxi driver could not drive me all the way to the temple because of the crowds and street vendors, but had to park a couple of blocks away and told me I needed to walk the rest of the way. I was somewhat confused in my crowded walk as I passed little souvenir stands everywhere that sold statues and pictures of the numerous Hindu gods. Animals and beggars surrounded me as we all pushed our way through the crowded streets. Many crippled people lay on the streets; women pushed their way towards me with outstretched hands, begging to feed their children. Children ran around, sometimes completely naked, squatting on the streets to relieve themselves. Animals scrounged through piles of garbage looking for something to eat, along with the hungry and destitute people. As I walked through these streets and saw such extreme poverty, desperation, and filth, I thought to myself, where are their gods? When I arrived at the temple, a man dressed in a white robe asked if he could show me around, but I knew he simply wanted me to pay him for his tour, so I declined; I would look around myself. He continued to follow me though, and almost demanded that he show me around the temple, so I grudgingly consented. Prayers were shouted in desperation to their gods, incense was burned, flowers were tossed into prayer bowls, and sacrifices were made. I saw and smelled the fresh blood of a goat that had recently been slaughtered in their sacrifice to the gods, where years ago, human sacrifices were made. I wondered why these worshippers still felt the need to sacrifice animals to appease their gods…

▌ What do you know about the sacrifice of Jesus on our behalf? _____

_____

_____

_____

_____

_____

▌ Do we still need to make sacrifices to appease God? _____
Why or why not? _____

_____

_____

_____

My "guide" took me to a place where I was told to remove my shoes. Next he tied a string around my wrist which he called a "prayer string," then told me to place the petal of a flower into a bowl, sign their book, and place money in the book for the poor at this sacred prayer spot of the temple. I realized the "poor" was my guide, and I did not like being lied to in this "sacred" spot. I explained that I was a Christian and was uncomfortable giving money to a Hindu temple, though he tried to assure me that my financial gift was alms for the poor, and suggested that I give a large contribution. I agreed to give a very small amount of money, turned and walked away to retrieve my shoes. I felt very empty and uneasy in that temple. I did not feel any peace in this place, but instead I felt chaos and desperation.

▌ Have you ever been anywhere or in a situation where you felt chaos and desperation rather than peace? _____

_____

▌ What were the circumstances surrounding that feeling? _____

_____

_____

▌ Could you have done anything to change that situation? _____

_____

_____

▌ What could you have done? _____

_____

_____

I also felt an absence of love and compassion. There were so many gods, and people were in a frantic desperation to please them. The faces of the people worshipping in the temple were empty. Their eyes were hollow and frightened.

▌ Why do you think people were so desperate? _____

_____

▌ Have you ever felt desperate, with no way out and nowhere to turn?
_____ What did you do? _____

_____

_____

▌ Do you have any regrets surrounding those desperate times, and today, would you have done anything differently? _____

_____

_____

_____

As I walked back to my taxi, I thought about how Christianity is the only religion where people do not desperately try to earn the favor and appeasement of God. Christianity is the only religion where, *"But God shows his love for us that while we were still sinners, Christ died for us"* (Romans 5:8). Christianity is the only religion where we do not have to earn our salvation, but we simply acknowledge the amazing gift we are offered through the death and resurrection of Jesus, and ask His Spirit to help us follow His perfect and loving blueprint for our lives. The Christian faith is quite beautiful, though living this life requires knowing the Bible, the Blueprint for our lives, so we do not get lost in narrow, crowded, busy streets of chaos and desperation, lost in the false temples of our own minds.

I know someone who has gone through recovery and has been clean and sober now for several years, doing very well. I was told that his "higher power" are horses and the beauty of the mountains and nature that now surround him as he manages a wild horse ranch. I am so very grateful for his successful recovery, but I worry that if for some reason he is taken out of his current environment and had to move away from the horses and mountains, he might fall back into a trap of addiction. Nature, horses, or any other "thing" in this world can become a god to us.

▮ Do you think there are false gods?_____

▮ Do you have any false gods?_____

▮ What are they?_____

_____

(Consider some of the things we spoke about in step one.)

▮ Is having God/Jesus as a Higher Power any different from something like nature or horses/animals? _____ Why or why not? _____

_____

_____

_____

Another one of my hospice patients out in Eastern Kentucky was named Dan. Although I was warned, I was still unprepared for what I saw. Dan was retaining fluid in his head for some reason that his doctors could not quite understand, and his head was twice its normal size. Dan's eyes were swollen shut, with the lids and surrounding skin about the size of golf balls. His lips were swollen and spread over his nose. He was a small, slight man who was quite thin, which seemed to exaggerate his swollen head and made it appear huge. I had never seen a human being look like this. When I got to the hospital to see him, I had to pretend that I was not shocked (though I was), and I also felt repulsed and sad, pitying this poor man. His girlfriend sat next to him in his bed, held his hand, and excitedly said, "Guess what? Dan is going to be baptized Sunday!" Dan told me on his first visit with him that he "wanted to get his life together before he died." Dan had seven children by four different women. His terminal illness was the result of thirty years of heavy drinking, smoking, and self-abuse. He began going to church a few months ago and the pastor showed him the Scripture that says, *"Repent and be baptized every one of you in the name of Jesus Christ for the forgiveness of your sins, and you will receive the gift of the Holy Spirit"* (Acts 2:38).

In Eastern Kentucky, if a person is going to be baptized, one must go to a creek and be submerged; that is the only way baptism is done there. Dan of course, had some medical conditions that needed to be discussed with his doctor and nurses, such as a feeding tube extending out from his stomach and a trachea tube in his throat; both of these areas were exposed and open, so there was concern for infection from the water. They decided to use gauze bandages, towels, and other precautions, in addition to telling the pastor to do a quick dunk! Dan was also very weak and needed assistance walking, so one of his son's helped him down to the creek. When I asked Dan about all of these potential dangers, he said that the Bible instructs us to believe and be baptized, so that was what he was going to do - period. Dan's baptism seemed almost like too much trouble with all of the precautions he needed to take. He also had a thirty minute drive to the creek, his eyes were swollen shut, his lips and throat were swollen and sore, he was sick, felt bad, and literally close to death. Why go through so much trouble?

▮ Have you ever felt you were supposed to do something, "the right thing," but it was too much trouble or an inconvenience to you? _____
_____

▮ Do you think you were more inconvenienced than Dan? _____
_____

▮ Do you think it is important to follow what the Bible says, even under such difficult circumstances? _____Why or Why not? _____
_____
_____

▮ Do you think that even though Dan lived a wild life ignoring God, that he was saved? _____ Why or why not? _____
_____
_____

■  Can anyone be saved? _____

Dan died a short time after his baptism.  Pictures of his baptism surrounded his coffin.  Dan could have lived a longer life had he not inflicted so much abuse upon himself, but near the end of his life, he realized there is indeed a God who loves us and has great mercy and compassion for us.  God loves us, forgives us, and reaches down to all of us, no matter what kind of lives we lead, to show us a better way.  God shows us His love through the Bible and through other Christ-followers.  None of us are too far from God's love and forgiveness.

■  Do you think there is anything in your life God cannot forgive? _____
■  Do you think everyone is given a chance for a "death-bed" conversion, or is it possible to die suddenly and never have the chance to turn our lives around? _____

*"Be not overly wicked, neither a fool.*
*Why should you die before your time?"*

(Ecclesiastes 7:17)

# Step Four:

## Begin To Develop A Christ-Centered Worldview

What does it mean to have a Christ-centered worldview? What is a worldview anyway? According to philosopher Robert Lehe, "Nearly everyone has a worldview that addresses issues of ultimate concern, no matter how carefully worked out or coherent it may be" (Lehe, p.9). Questions in our worldview are topics such as: Why does the universe exist? Does my life have purpose? Is there a God? How should I live my life? "A worldview articulates, among other things, assumptions about the nature of the world, the ultimate *telos* (meaning or purpose) of human existence (or lack thereof), and the basic values by which one should live. Worldviews are philosophical frameworks that organize one's beliefs about ultimate questions of existence, meaning, and value" (Lehe, p. 9).

- ▌ Have you ever thought about your worldview? _____ (We will define and discuss this more).
- ▌ Have you considered what meaning or purpose there is to your life, or even if there is any? _____
- ▌ Do you have clear values and ethics, things you should or should not do, and adhere to those values each day? _____

Religion and belief (or disbelief) in God fall into our worldviews. Many people who do not believe in God, or at least adhere to any religion or practice in the worship of God, do not believe because of the enormity of human suffering in the world. How can a good God allow so much suffering? While there is some suffering in this world caused by nature, such as death and destruction from storms, floods, tornadoes, hurricanes, etc., and tragedies such as childhood diseases, "a large portion of human suffering is the result of morally bad human behavior" (Lehe, p. 10). Do you agree?

▌ What does suffering say about human nature? _____

_____

_____

▌ What do the problems with human nature say about our need for God?

_____

_____

▌ What would a world that has no God look like? _____

_____

_____

▌ What is the purpose of human beings being on this earth? _____

_____

_____

▌ What is the purpose of your life in particular? _____

_____

_____

Christians, or people who have a Christ-centered worldview, believe there is pain and suffering in the world due to sin.  The Bible says the whole creation groans and feels the effects of sin (Romans 8:21-22), which is why nature also is subject to death, and there are natural disasters such as floods, tornadoes, hurricanes, earthquakes, etc.  Sin is only possible because God gave us free will; we can choose to live according to His laws and love Him, or we can choose to do our own thing and not care about Him and His laws, which is sin, and which results in chaos and confusion.  God gave us free will because He did not want to force us to love Him, just like we do not want to force others to love us, but rather, we want love to flow naturally.

In my trip to India, I began to realize how much Mother Teresa and the Missionaries of Charity had developed a Christ-centered worldview, which brought beauty to the world and great purpose to their lives.  Mother Teresa lived in this dirty, smelly, poverty-stricken city because she wanted dying people to know there is a God who loves them, and that people who love this God, Jesus, also love and care for all people, mostly the forgotten people in society or anyone who is often overlooked or looked down upon.  In the Bible, the apostle Paul wrote about Jesus, "*For in Him we live, and move, and have our being*" (Acts 17:28).  A Christ-centered worldview involves God in every area of our lives.

When I first arrived in Calcutta, I saw so many people in rags, and babies and small children literally naked.  I felt uneasy about the huge suitcase I brought with my clothes, basically a different outfit for each day, and the closet full of clothes I still had at home.  I also thought about the words of Jesus as recorded in Scripture that says, "*For I was hungry and you gave me no food... naked and you did not clothe me... Truly I tell you, just as you did not do it to one of the least of these, you did not do it to Me*" (Matthew 25).

▌ If we claim to love God, what is our obligation to other people? _____

_____

_____

▌ What is our obligation to ourselves? _____

_____

_____

▌ How do we love our neighbor as ourselves if we do not love or care for ourselves? _____

_____

_____

While in Calcutta, I met a woman from Australia who was also traveling alone, so one night we decided to find somewhere to eat dinner together. Many street children approached us begging for money, but the Sisters at the Missionaries of Charity had warned us not to give them any money since it perpetuates their sad lives.  The street children are run by the mafia in Calcutta who take the children's money anyway.  These evil men of the mafia often maim the children so people feel stronger pity for them and give them more money; this is truly suffering caused by sinful, immoral behavior, by people who have no concept of God or any idea of a worldview that sees human beings as beautiful and created in the image of God.  Actions like those of the mafia are part of what a world without God would look like.

Developing a Christ-centered worldview does not happen overnight.  If we view the world as Christ does, and we see ourselves and other people as beautiful creations made in the image of God, this worldview can at least begin.  When the world revolves around ourselves, when we live selfishly or with anger, unforgiveness, or bitterness, we definitely do not have a Christ-centered worldview, and are stuck with a world view that leaves God out.

When I was working as a hospice chaplain in rural Eastern Kentucky, I met some people who had an amazing worldview that focused on Christ and His love and forgiveness.  There was not a trace of bitterness or anger in these people, where, for most of us, we would probably think was justified.  I drove to Ken and Pat's house and had to park at the top of a steep, winding, gravel hill, then walk several blocks down to their tiny old wooden house.  I laughed at the old toilets outside that now served as flower pots, and watched the chickens, dogs, and cats run around the yard, past the cars that sat up on blocks waiting for repair. When I got to the door, I knocked and was told to come in from a voice inside.  In the living room, my hospice patient lay in a hospital bed surrounded by attentive family.  There was no air conditioning, and the room was very hot and stuffy. Even in this heat, Pat was trying to lift a blanket to cover her dying husband Ken, but was having some difficulty.  I noticed three of the fingers on her left hand were gone; only her thumb and pinkie remained.  She noticed that I looked at her hand and said, "It's hard sometimes with this hand.  I got all of my fingers blown off with a shotgun" she said in a matter-of-fact manner.  "What?" I asked in surprise! "Oh, his father" (pointing to her husband), "shot at us with a shotgun. I put my hand up to protect my husband as I tried to close the door and got my fingers blown away.  He got hit in the neck – see the scar?" She pointed to his neck.  I could barely believe what I was hearing.

"Tell me about this Pat" I said.

"Well, he just came after us with a shotgun, that's all" (as if this is a normal event I thought!).

I asked the obvious question, "Why?"

"Oh, because his wife told him to; she said, 'shoot the SOB!' He was afraid of his wife, so he did whatever she told him. She was mean."

I then asked, "She said that about her own son? Her birth son?"

"Yes" Pat replied. I was astonished. Pat told this story as if it was something normal, and Ken said nothing.

"What happened after that? Were you afraid? Did you call the police?" I was filled with questions!

"No, they never came after us again. I was sure they wouldn't. He came to us later and asked for our forgiveness."

"Did you forgive him?" I asked.

Pat did not hesitate for a moment and said, "Of course! I asked him if he asked the Lord for forgiveness, and he said he did, so if God could forgive him, then I must too."

"Did Ken forgive his dad?" I asked.

"Yes."

"What about his mother, who told his father to shoot him. Did he forgive her?"

"Oh, she never asked us for forgiveness, but we both forgave her. We actually didn't see her until she was dying. I held her hand as she died."

I was so amazed at this story of forgiveness that was offered so freely. The Bible says we must forgive, and God freely forgives us when we ask, so Pat and Ken simply forgave; they both truly developed a Christ-centered worldview.

▋ Could you forgive someone, especially someone like your parents (or spouse or children) if they did something so terrible to you? _____

▌ Why or why not? _____

_____

_____

▌ If we learn to develop a Christ-centered worldview, must we forgive, even terrible things done to us? _____

_____

_____

▌ As Jesus was being nailed to the Cross, He said, *"Father forgive them, for they don't know what they are doing."* What do you think of that kind of forgiveness? _____

_____

_____

As we leave this fourth step, think about your worldview and how it affects your life.  Ask yourself the questions again about just what a worldview is, and then consider your own.

*"And forgive us our debts, as we also have forgiven our debtors"*
(Matthew 6:12 – a portion of The Lord's Prayer)

# Step Five:

## Learn To See God In Daily Life

I often hear people say they are thankful for just waking up in the morning or, more specifically, that "God woke them up." I am indeed thankful each morning, not only that I woke up, but also when I take my dog for a run, that I am healthy and able to do so. I acknowledge that it is God who has blessed me with good health, at least for now. God has blessed me with a home, food, family, and friends. There are many simple things that we take for granted, but they are all truly blessings from God, which we need to see in our daily lives.

When I was in India, I had no idea what to expect as far as my accommodations. I had a small but clean room, and I was most grateful that I had a toilet, sink, and shower; I had no idea if I would even have running water. When I opened the shutters and looked out of my hotel window each morning, I saw naked children bathing at a water pump in the street. I know many people in the world have never, and will never know what it is like to take a hot shower and feel water sprinkle down on them. I know many people have never, and will never know what it is like to lay down on a mattress at night, pull a sheet and blanket over their body, and rest their head on a soft pillow. I also know many people in the world have never, and will never have the "luxury" of turning on a light and having electricity, or being able to go to a sink and drink clean water. These daily "luxuries" that we take for granted are truly gifts from God that many people in the world will never experience. Looking around at the people in India caused me to think about these blessings even more, and to see the grace and mercy of God in simple, everyday life.

■ Do you ever stop to thank God for what you have, even if it is not a lot?

▌ A simple prayer before eating a meal is a good reminder of gratefulness. Do you give thanks before you eat? _____

▌ While walking through the crowded, dirty streets of Calcutta, or looking out of my window at the naked children bathing at the water pump, or rummaging through the garbage for food, can God still be seen? Can God only be seen in the beauty and goodness of life, or can we see Him everywhere? _____

Some people do not believe in God because of the pain and suffering in the world. When I was young adult, on my own, I was very poor. Life was difficult and I had to work very, very hard, six days a week to support my son and me. I was not nearly as poor as these people in India, but I was indeed poor. Jesus said, *"For you will always have the poor with you"* (Matthew 26:11). So how do we learn to see God when daily life is often so difficult? I see God in the faces of the Missionaries of Charity, and in all people who try to relieve the suffering that is a part of this world. When I walked into the home for the dying in Calcutta, I saw God in the Sisters who bathed these dying people, who fed them, touched them, prayed for them, and simply sat with them as they died. God can be seen, in simple acts of love.

One of my patients in eastern Kentucky was a man named Larry. He was totally bedbound, and could not move his body very much because of advanced Parkinson's disease. When Larry's third wife discovered he was dying, she left him. Larry was of course, very angry, compounded by the fact that his two sons rarely visited. Larry's three wives and two sons abandoned him, and his body failed him. Larry's sister Sandy took him into her modest home to care for him. Sandy lived in a small single-wide trailer in the middle of a "yard" of mud. There were no grassy areas, no flowers, no bushes, and no trees. The only thing that surrounded their home was mud. Larry's life consisted of lying in bed, looking out a picture window at the mud, and having his sister care for him. Sandy's friend, Randy, hung a hummingbird feeder outside in Larry's field of vision to give him something of beauty to look at during his long days. Perhaps God could be seen in the beauty of nature: hummingbirds and the kindness of Randy.

One day when Sandy was frying some potatoes, a grease fire broke out. The flames quickly spread and the trailer began to melt. Larry could not breathe well because of his disease, so he always wore an oxygen mask. The fire should have caused his oxygen to explode, but it did not. Sandy and Randy quickly fled the house and called the fire department; they tried to rescue Larry, but they could not reach him. Larry could not move and called out to his panicked sister, but the heat and the flames prevented her from reaching him. Flames engulfed the trailer. When the fire department arrived, Sandy told them her brother was still inside, but they told her he must already be dead with the thick black smoke and flames everywhere. Randy and Sandy could not accept this statement from the firemen, so she broke the window near Larry's bed, then Randy pulled the oxygen mask off of Larry and dragged him through the broken window. Despite the fact that the hospital bed was half melted, the television completely burned, as well as everything else in Larry's room, he was totally unharmed, without a scratch, bruise, burn, or singe!

Larry's miraculous protection reminded me of the story in the Bible, found in Daniel chapter 3. King Nebuchadnezzar had commanded everyone in Babylon to worship a huge golden statue that he had erected. Three men, Shadrach, Meshach, and Abednego, refused to worship this statue because they said they would only worship God. Nebuchadnezzar was furious, and said if there was anyone who would not worship his golden statue, they would be thrown into a blazing hot furnace. The three men who refused, told the king, "*If this be so, our God whom we serve is able to deliver us from the burning fiery furnace*" (Daniel 3:17). Because of their refusal to obey the evil command of the king, they were tied up and thrown into the furnace. King Nebuchadnezzar looked into the furnace and said, "*I see four men unbound, walking in the midst of the fire, and they are not hurt; and the appearance of the fourth is like a son of the gods*" (Daniel 3:25). The fourth "person" was an angel.

- ▌ Do you believe Larry might have been saved by an angel?_____
- ▌ Do you believe God had something to do with Larry's survival? _____

As Sandy told me this story of the fire, I asked Larry if he was in a panic at the time, and I could not imagine how he must have felt. Larry calmly said, "No. I heard a voice tell me that I would be alright, and then I felt a hand surround me and protect me from the flames. I knew it was God." Larry said he previously was not a believer, though he was an avid reader of the Bible. He rarely went to church, and he described himself as a, "mean woman chaser and a wild sinner." Through this experience with the fire, Larry knew God was giving him another chance, perhaps his last and final chance at salvation. Larry knew he was dying, and he was immensely thankful that God spared him from the fire in order to entrust himself to Jesus before he died. In the midst of the worst and most frightening experience of being bedbound in the middle of a fire, Larry saw the hand of God and His incredible grace and mercy, even to a mean woman chaser and wild sinner. Larry said at this time, nearing the end of his life, that God transformed him into a nice, calm man who was no longer angry at the world and everyone around him, and that he was now "a new person since Jesus came into his life." Larry, Sandy, and Randy truly saw God in their daily lives.

▌ Why do you think God would care about such a mean, angry, sinful man like Larry? _____

_____

▌ Do you believe this story that Sandy told me about the fire? _____ Why or why not? _____

_____

_____

▌ How does accepting the love of Jesus change people? _____

_____

_____

_____

▌ Do you see God in your daily life, even if things are not as dramatic as a house fire? _____

▌ How do you see God? _____

_____

_____

▌ Have you ever had a dramatic or frightening experience where you saw God's "hand" save you? _____ Please share your stories.

When I was eighteen years old, I was driving through a very poor part of Chicago where I lived.  While I was sitting at a stop light, I heard glass breaking. I remember thinking, "What was that?" To my horror, it was three men breaking my car windows with baseball bats and 2 x 4's, as I sat there with nowhere to go since there was a car in front of me and behind me.  The men grabbed my backpack, which included pretty much everything I owned, including my driver's license and money.  My back window, front windshield, and passenger side windows were all broken out.  When I tell people this story, most people ask, "Why wasn't your driver's side window broken?" If it had been, surely I would have been smashed in the head as well, and possibly killed.  I simply respond, it was God's "hand" protecting me.  I was pregnant at the time, and if I had been killed, my son would have never been born, nor my granddaughter, nor the future generations that will come through her.  I did not know Jesus at that time either; so, like Larry, God gave me another chance at salvation.

▌ Has God given you another chance at life? _____
▌ What are you doing with that opportunity? _____

_____

_____


*"Look at the birds of the air; they neither sow nor reap*
*nor gather into barns, and yet your heavenly Father feeds them"*
(Matthew 6:26).

*When we take our mind off ourself
and focus on others, God can begin to help.*

# Step Six:

## Deny Yourself For The Sake Of Loving Others

One of the most amazing people I have ever heard of is Mother Teresa. She was the ultimate example of denying yourself for the sake of loving others. Mother Teresa was born and raised in Skopje, Yugoslavia (now Macedonia). As a young woman, Mother Teresa worked in India, where she witnessed great poverty and need. For many years, Mother Teresa taught at a wealthy girl's school in Calcutta, India that was run by the sisters (nuns) of Loreto, a Catholic order she joined when she was just eighteen years old. When Mother Teresa was 36 years old, on a train ride to Darjeeling, India, she said, "I sensed a call to renounce everything in order to follow Christ in the poor suburbs, to serve amongst the poorest of the poor" (Mother Teresa, p.146). Mother Teresa had an unwavering desire to start what would be the Missionaries of Charity in Calcutta, after sensing this "call" on her life. She wanted to leave the sisters of Loreto and her teaching work at the school, because she believed Jesus was telling her to find Indian nuns to help her to, "radiate his love to the poorest of the poor, the sick, the dying and the street children" (Poplin, p. 31). As a Catholic nun, she needed permission to leave her order and start this ministry to the poorest of the poor. Her request was initially denied, so for almost two years, she fought for her vision to work with the street people, because she felt it was God's specific call on her life. Finally, her request was granted. Alone, she went and received some medical training, then went into the slums of Calcutta to begin her work. Two years later, the Missionaries of Charity were officially established.

▌ Do you feel any "call" or purpose to your life? _____

_____

_____

_____

▌ What are you doing to make this call/ purpose a reality? _____

_____

_____

▌ Do you think everyone has a "call" or purpose to their lives? _____

_____

▌ Do you think Mother Teresa's "call" or purpose required great sacrifice?

_____

▌ Why or why not? _____

_____

▌ Why is sacrifice important, or is it? _____

_____

▌ What does sacrifice look like? _____

_____

Over the years, thousands of people have volunteered at the Missionaries of Charity in Calcutta, including myself.  In order to volunteer with these nuns, you cannot just show up and work.  You need to write a letter of request and be accepted.  Mary Poplin, a woman who wrote a book about her time volunteering in Calcutta, wrote her letter asking to come and work, and she also asked what she would need to bring on her trip.  Her response from Sister Priscilla, who was in charge of the volunteers, said, "Come with a heart of love and hands to serve Jesus in the crippled, the abandoned, the sick and dying in any one of our centres" (Poplin, p. 10).

There are multiple places to serve at the Missionaries of Charity in Calcutta, such as the home for the dying (where I served), a children's home for orphans, a leper colony, as well as other places of need.  Here in America, some of us might volunteer as nursery workers at a church, or Sunday school teachers, maybe a soup kitchen or with the Red Cross, but volunteering in Calcutta was unlike any place I had ever been; it was depressing, dirty, smelly, and hellish.  I was in Calcutta for two weeks, and on my last day there, I could not even leave my hotel room.  I had enough of the misery.  I remain amazed that Mother Teresa CHOSE to live and work there, despite being told no for almost two years.  So why did she practically beg her superiors to allow her to set up the Missionaries of Charity in such an awful place? Because she believed God told her to do so, and rather than consider her own comforts and desires, she wanted to obey God, deny herself, and love others.  Mother Teresa said, "We must know exactly when we say *yes* to God what is in that *yes*.  *Yes* means "I surrender," totally, fully, without any counting the cost, without any examination: Is it alright? Is it convenient? Our *yes* to God is without any reservations… Total surrender to God must come in small details as it comes in big details" (Mother Teresa, p. 148).

∎ Have you ever "surrendered" yourself (did not think of yourself) even when it was inconvenient or difficult? _____

_____

∎ What is our natural reaction to being part of another's pain and suffering?

_____

_____

∎ Have you ever denied yourself drugs, alcohol, or some other addiction or bad behavior for the sake of a loved one, such as a parent, spouse, or child? _____

_____

∎ What do you think Mother Teresa meant when she said we must surrender to God even the small details? _____

_____

_____

When I worked as a hospice chaplain here in the States, I was often privileged to experience the best in people when I watched them deny themselves for the sake of loving and caring for others.  It is truly amazing and beautiful to witness people draw from strength they did not even know they had, to help their loved ones who were very ill and dying.  One day I drove deep into a hollow in the Appalachian Mountains to visit Ann, the primary care-giver and daughter of her mother Clara, who had died the previous day.  I wanted to see how Ann was dealing with the death of her mother since she had been so close to her and had taken care of her for so long.  Ann met me on the porch with a smile and a strong hug, pulled up two rocking chairs for us, then went into the kitchen for iced tea. We sat in silence for a while as we rocked, drinking our tea and watching the horses in the fields in front of us. Ann began to talk about her mom and how difficult it was taking care of her as she slowly died. Ann said though, that she had no regrets.

I think living without regrets is important. We all have regrets from mistakes we made in the past, but beginning now, maybe we can live without regrets. What amazed me about Ann, was her humility and her strength. She said, "I had no idea what I was doing half the time, taking care of mom. People asked me how I did it, and I said, 'I don't know; you just do what you do!' Remember I used to tell you when you came to visit mom that I didn't know what to do sometimes? But God gives you what you need when you need it. He's got it goin' on! He's an awesome God!" Ann lovingly denied herself, her sleep, her time, and her comforts for the sake of loving her mother. Ann had no regrets. Do you?

■ Are you able to sacrifice your desires for the sake of loving others, even when it is very inconvenient and difficult? _____

_____

■ Step six of AA says, "Were entirely ready to have God remove all these defects of character." What might be a defect of character that prevents us from denying ourselves for the sake of loving others? _____

_____

_____

Whatever difficulties we face in life, God can give us the strength we need to overcome the challenges or temptations, like He did with Ann. When we take our mind off ourselves and focus on others, God can begin to help. The Christian faith does not call just the "super Christians" like Mother Teresa, Billy Graham, or Jesus' disciples to deny themselves for the sake of the Gospel and others, but the Bible calls ALL people to live in this manner. Mark 8:34 says, *"And calling the crowd to him with his disciples, he"* (Jesus) *"said to them, 'If anyone would come after me, let him deny himself and take up his cross and follow me. For whoever would save his life will lose it, but whoever loses his life for my sake and the gospel's will save it."*

■  What do you think Jesus meant in that quote above? (re-read it slowly)

_____

_____

_____

■  When we deny ourselves for the sake of loving others, does that make us more loving people? Stronger people? Less selfish people? _____

_____

_____

**"Do nothing out of rivalry or conceit, but in humility consider others
as more important than yourselves"**

(Philippians 2:3).

*"As a rule, when we are suffering, we are so focused on ourselves we have no time for others... remain as empty as possible, so that God can fill you"*

Mother Teresa

# Step Seven:

## Allow Jesus To Be More, And Yourself To Be Less

A strange thing occurred one evening when I was in Calcutta. After work one day, I decided to go to dinner with a woman I met at my hotel. She was from Australia doing Ph.D. research, also traveling alone. As we walked to the restaurant where we chose to eat, many street children approached my friend begging for money. Since we had previously been warned not to give them any money, she politely refused; the children never approached me. Next, a man approached my friend as we continued our walk and began a conversation with her. He was one of the many shop- owners who followed and harassed foreigners, as he begged travelers to buy items from his shop. She politely brushed him off and he finally walked away; the man never approached me. When we arrived at the restaurant, the waiter greeted my friend and handed her a menu; he did not acknowledge me. My friend looked at the waiter and asked, "Could you get my friend a menu too?" After dinner, we walked to a little café for a cup of tea and desert, and, once again, I was ignored as if I were not even visible! I was not spoken to nor given a menu there either. My friend was asked what she wanted to order, but I was not asked. At this point, my friend and I discussed this strange on-going occurrence and we simply left the café – without tea or desert.

When we returned to our hotel that evening, we laughed together about how I must have become invisible that night, which we did not understand. My friend was an average, middle-aged woman, and there was nothing particular about her appearance that would have made her stand out amongst me or any other person; it was perplexing.

▌ Have you ever felt ignored and invisible? _____

▌ How did you feel when you were not acknowledged? _____
_____

▌ What were the circumstances surrounding your "invisibility?" _____
_____
_____

▌ Why does it bother us so much to feel "invisible?" _____
_____
_____

▌ What does that say about human nature? _____
_____
_____

In her work in Calcutta with the Missionaries of Charity, Mother Teresa once said, "*As a rule, when we are suffering, we are so focused on ourselves we have no time for others… remain as empty as possible, so that God can fill you*" (Poplin, p. 126).

▌ How do we empty ourselves? _____
_____
_____

▌ What do we empty ourselves of in order for God to fill us? _____
_____
_____

In the previous step (Step Six), I spoke about Ann, that strong woman who took such good care of her mom Clara before she passed away. Clara was also an amazing woman who I loved to visit. Clara and Ann lived together in an old home, on more acres than I could see, at the end of a long, dirt road. Their home was tucked into the Appalachian Mountains and was built on a large, green field surrounded by horses and vegetable gardens. Creeks ran through their property, and the sound of trickling water over the rocks was beautiful and calming. Their old farm house was large, clean, and well-kept, and they made me feel very comfortable each time I visited. Ann and Clara always offered me a cup of coffee or tea when I arrived and were wonderful hostesses. Both mother and daughter were quiet, polite, and humble, and neither ever appeared to think of themselves.

Each time I visited Clara, I told her how much I admired her faith and her strength. Clara suffered from oral cancer and was usually in some pain. She often held a damp washcloth against her swollen face for comfort. One particular day while I was visiting, I asked Clara about her pain and how she was dealing with it. Clara's response amazed me. She said, "its o.k. I will never suffer as Jesus did for us when He hung on the Cross, so I can't complain." I was dumbfounded, and I told her how much I respected her faith and her courage. She just shrugged and smiled at me, as if her comment was nothing unusual.

- If you are dealing with any pain right now, either emotional, spiritual, or physical, do you think you could have the same attitude as Clara? _____

  _____

- Why or why not? _____

  _____

  _____

- What characteristics or particular strengths does it take to minimize your own pain in light of the physical, emotional, and spiritual pain that Jesus suffered on our behalf? _____

  _____

  _____

  _____

I also told Clara that I was amazed each time I visited, that she was always so considerate. Clara always offered me something to eat or drink, asked if I was comfortable where I sat, and when I read to her from the Bible, she asked if I had enough light. She always wanted to know how I was doing that day and asked about my family. Here was this dying woman, in pain, yet she consistently showed concern for me, a total stranger (other than her hospice chaplain), as well as concern for her daughter, Ann, and anyone else I saw who came to visit.

Most healthy people are not even that considerate and selfless! Clara considered her suffering minimal since she compared it to the sufferings of Jesus, her Lord and Savior.

▌ How do you feel when you are around people who never think of themselves, but only of others? _____

_____

▌ When we are in any kind of pain, either physical or emotional, is it difficult or easy to think of others rather than ourselves? _____

_____

▌ Why does pain of any kind dominate our thoughts and hinder us from considering other people? _____

_____

▌ How can we break free from self-absorption and think more of others than we do ourselves? _____

_____

Let's read Philippians 2:5-11:

*"Have this mind among yourselves, which is yours in Christ Jesus, who, though He was in the form of God, did not consider equality with God a thing to be grasped, but emptied Himself, by taking the form of a servant, being born in the likeness of men. And being found in human form, He humbled Himself by becoming obedient to the point of death, even death on a cross. Therefore, God has highly exalted Him and bestowed on him the name that is above every name, so that at the name of Jesus every knee should bow, in heaven and on earth and under the earth, and every tongue confess that Jesus Christ is Lord, to the glory of God the Father."*

▌ How do you feel about what Jesus did in this Scripture? _____

_____

_____

_____

■ If we are supposed to be Christ-like, how can we live our lives? _____

_____

_____

_____

■ Was Clara Christ-like? _____ How? _____

_____

_____

_____

*"He must increase, but I must decrease"*

(John 3:30).

*Learning is a process.*

# Step Eight:

## Learn To Love, Help, And Live Selflessly

On one of the first days that our volunteer group began working in Kalighat (the home of the dying), many people had great emotional and spiritual difficulties as a result of the poor conditions of the city and the very few and basic "necessities" these poor Indian people possessed. The sick men were on one side of the building with male volunteers, while the women patients were on the other side with female volunteers. Each patient slept on a cot instead of a bed like most of the volunteers were used to, with many, many cots in the one large room for the sick and dying people. Alone and sometimes terrified, we watched women being brought in, literally off the streets, to be cared for and either nursed back to health, or more often, to die in peace and relative comfort, in the presence of people who cared for them. The Sisters did not want anyone to die alone.

I watched one particular volunteer sit with a tiny, dying, malnourished woman who just sat and cried most of the time. The volunteer also began to cry. I walked over and sat down next to these two women, and the volunteer, who was also from America said to me, "This is just too much! I can't handle this place… these people… it's so awful!" I gently put my arm around her and said, "Yes, I know, it is awful. But you are here with this woman, and you are Jesus to her at this moment." The volunteer smiled and held the woman close to her side. I thought of Matthew 25 where Jesus said,

"*Come, you that are blessed by My Father, inherit the kingdom prepared for you from the foundation of the world. For I was hungry and you gave me food, I was thirsty and you gave me drink, I was a stranger and you welcomed me, I was naked and you clothed me, I was sick and you visited me, I was in prison and you came to me…Truly I say to you, as you did it to one of the least of these my brothers, you did it to me"* (Matthew 25:34-36 & 40).

The work in Kalighat was not easy – physically, emotionally, mentally, or spiritually.  I only worked in Calcutta for two weeks and witnessed the misery of this place.  Mother Teresa and the Missionaries of Charity worked there day in and day out.  The only way a person could do this work for so many years is if they did indeed learn to love, help, and live selflessly, without their own comforts in mind, or as their priority.

▮ What comforts of your own could you give up for others? (Think about your addictions or bad habits/weaknesses that hurt your loved ones) ___

_____

_____

_____

▮ The Scripture above referred to physical help in caring for other people. What are some emotional or mental things we can sacrifice in order to show love to others? (Think about anger, bitterness, unforgiveness, etc.)

_____

_____

_____

Day after day the other volunteers and I came to Kalighat to help and to love these dying women.  We washed their clothes and sheets by hand in big tubs on the floor and hung them up to dry.  We exercised the ladies limbs and tried to help them move or walk.  We massaged their arms and legs with oil to ease their pains.  We held their hands and smiled.  We fed them and gave them something to drink.  We spoke in languages they could not understand, but at least they knew they were spoken to.  Our smiles, our touch, and our presence though, were understood.  I wish I could say that I wanted to remain in Kalighat and work, but I cannot.  I hated Calcutta: the noise, the smells, the crowds, the constant begging, and the sheer misery and poverty of that place.  I wanted to go back to my own quiet home, my warm and clean bed, American food, and the normal comforts of my life.

▎ Do you find it easier to satisfy yourself and enjoy your own comforts, even at the expense of others? _____ Give an example: _____

_____

_____

▎ Why is it important that we learn to live selflessly? _____

_____

_____

▎ Does human nature wish to live for ourselves, or for other people? _____

_____

_____

Working in Kalighat felt like the ultimate hospice to me, especially since back home, I worked as a hospice chaplain. One of my patient's back home was an old man named Ivan. He lived in a narrow, deep hollow in the Appalachian Mountains in a tiny wooden house with one of his sons. The house was usually dirty, but Ivan's daughter and a neighbor came by about once a week to clean. Ivan was bed-bound, so his hospital bed was in the living room next to a large picture window that looked out at the mountains. Ivan was usually depressed with his inability to walk or do much of anything except watch the birds and the leaves blow in the wind, and listen to the ticking of the clock on the wall.

When I first met Ivan, he was a very crabby and unhappy man who did not want anyone to bother him. I gently persisted in visiting, and finally broke through! Eventually, primarily out of boredom I suppose, Ivan looked forward to my visits, which I grew to enjoy. Ivan was 92 years old, and he told me that at age 89 he was baptized in a creek, in his wheelchair! He told me that he, "heard a voice, I think it was the Lord, who told me if I got baptized that I would walk again. Well, you saw those pictures; I got baptized, and I haven't walked since! I guess maybe it wasn't the Lord after all since He doesn't lie... but I sure thought it was." I looked at Ivan for a minute and said, "Maybe it was the Lord, and maybe He meant that you will indeed walk again, but in Heaven."

▌ Have you ever thought God "told" you something, but it did not appear to go the way you thought? _____

_____

▌ Do you think there are times when God does not keep His word? _____

_____

▌ Do you think as humans, we can easily misunderstand God? _____

_____

Ivan began to cry. "I have a lot of dreams you know" he said. "I had a dream that I was walking all over this house, and then I began to walk in the clouds. Maybe you're right. I know there's a place in the Bible that says we'll get new bodies." I walked over to a table that held a huge Bible and read to Ivan from 1 Corinthians 15 where it talks about getting new bodies after we die that will be imperishable, for those of us who are saved. Ivan cried some more, and said even if he never walked again, he wanted all people to be saved and for everyone to have new bodies. He said, "But I know in order for me and others to get a new body, we must believe and follow Christ. I just wish all people knew Him. I do believe every word in that Bible!"

▌ Do you think Ivan was learning to love and live selflessly?_____ Why or why not? _____

_____

▌ Is it ever too late to learn to love, help and live selflessly? _____

_____

_____

▌ What is holding you back from living this way? _____

_____

_____

_____

*"For to me to live is Christ, and to die is gain"*

(Philippians 1:21).

*God does not desire to make our lives miserable,*
*but Jesus said He came to give life, and*
*to give it abundantly and fully.*

# Step Nine:

## Understand Your Will As It Conflicts With God's Will

As I have previously mentioned, while I loved the work in Calcutta, the camaraderie I had with other volunteers from around the world, and just being at Mother Teresa's home for the dying, I did not like living in Calcutta at all, and I was anxious to go home. I met several volunteers who came to Calcutta every year for their "vacation," or who spend long periods of time working with the Missionaries of Charity. I thought, "What if God wants me to work here for a long period of time, or even move here?" Would I say "No" to God?

▎ Have you ever thought God was calling you to do something that you did not want to do? _____

▎ Maybe God was telling you to stop a behavior, habit, or addiction, and you did not want to stop. How would that affect your relationship with God? _____

_____

▎ Have you ever felt like God was telling you to forgive someone, or to ask forgiveness from someone, even reconcile a relationship, and you refused? _____

▎ What does our disobedience do to our souls? _____

_____

_____

In the Bible, Jesus said, "*If anyone would come after me, let him deny himself and take up his cross daily and follow me*" (Luke 9:23).

▎ What does it mean to deny yourself? _____

_____

■   Have you ever denied yourself on a daily basis? _____

_____

I thought, if God told me to move to Calcutta and live there for years, or even for the rest of my life on earth, could I deny the comforts of my own home in America? I realized that it is easy for my own will to conflict with God's will (which is probably true for most, if not all people). God does not desire to make our lives miserable, but Jesus said He came to give life, and to give it abundantly and fully (John 10:10). God does indeed desire to give us good things, which He often does. I am from the Chicago area, but I love the mountains. God opened up an opportunity for me to move to the Appalachian Mountains to work as a chaplain. When the solitude became too much for me, He opened up another job for me so that I could move somewhere else (which is the place where I met my husband!) God knew I wanted to see Mother Teresa's work in Calcutta, and He enabled me to travel there. Psalm 37:4 says, *"Delight yourself in the Lord, and he will give you the desires of your heart."* I have seen God do that over and over again in my life.

■   What are the desires of your heart? _____

_____

_____

■   Do you think God can grant you those desires? _____
■   Has He done so in the past? _____

God may test us though, to see if we are serious about our commitment to Him, to our word, and to other people. If we want to see God work in our lives, we must first be open to Him and His love, ask Him for the strength to live in ways that we know are right, and be willing to go through some trials to prepare us for the good things God has in store for us. The trials though, are difficult and usually conflict with our own will. With my own struggle of serving the "poorest of the poor" in the dirty, crowded, and noisy slums of Calcutta, and my desire to be home in the peace and quiet of my own clean home, I realized how strongly my will usually conflicts with God's will.

Back home in Kentucky, I went to visit a man named Bob, who suffered terribly from bone cancer.  Shortly after I arrived, Bob was taken by ambulance to the hospital in a pain-crisis.  Bob had been a pastor for twenty years, and even through his physical suffering, He never questioned God or lost his faith.  Years ago, Bob's oldest son was killed in a car accident.  The rescue workers believed their son had a heart attack before he crashed, and when they arrived at the scene, they were all brought to their knees in tears and prayer.  Bob's wife said they told her their son died with a smile on his face, clutching a Bible.  Bob's wife said if their son's death caused other people to believe in Jesus, then some good came out of it.

- Have you ever doubted God's goodness, or even His existence when you suffered in some way or saw a loved one suffer?_____
- How can we reconcile suffering with a good and loving God?  _____

_____

_____

(That has been a question for thousands of years, called a *theodicy* – reconciling the goodness of God with evil and suffering in the world).

- Do you think it's possible as human beings that we may never understand God or why He allows suffering? _____
- Do you think good can come out of suffering? _____

_____

- Do you think if God is good, He is the cause of suffering? _____
  If not, who or what is the cause? _____

_____

_____

Shortly after this tragedy of losing his son, Bob did not feel well and he thought he was suffering from his grief.  Bob continued to feel worse, and went to his doctor, who was also his friend.  His doctor told him that he was indeed suffering from grief and from pain from a previous mining accident where Bob was crushed and nearly died.  As time went by, Bob continued to feel worse, and he asked his doctor if he could see a specialist; his doctor never made the referral. About a year later, Bob's pain greatly increased and he was much sicker. He finally got a referral, and it was discovered that Bob had stage-four bone cancer. Bob was declared terminal; he would soon die.

▌ Bob never expressed anger at his doctor for not giving him the referral to the specialist earlier. Would you be angry? _____

▌ Bob told me that his other son asked him one day how to know if you are really a Christian or not. How do we know? _____
_____
_____

Bob gave a very simple, yet profound answer to his son's question: he said, "You know you are a Christian and are following Jesus when your greatest desire is to follow His will, despite your own desires, and that you love others more than you love yourself. That's how you know." Bob was able to live in God's will, even when it conflicted with his own will; a very difficult thing to do.

*"I have been crucified with Christ. It is no longer I who live,*
*but Christ who lives in me."*

(Galatians 2:20)

# Step Ten:

## Learn To Trust, Love, And Obey God Completely

My travels to Calcutta, India, took almost thirty hours, including the actual time in the planes and the layovers between flights. When I finally arrived in India, went through customs, and obtained my luggage, I was exhausted. Traveling alone, half-way around the world with no one to meet me at the airport, unsure of where my hotel was located, I thought I surely needed to trust God to keep me safe and give me the wherewithal to know what I was doing and where I was going, especially landing in India at night. At the airport, I shared a taxi with a fellow, solo American traveler to my hotel, which took close to an hour. My new American "friend" made sure I got into my hotel safely, and agreed to pay extra fare to travel to my hotel, even though his hotel was on the other side of town. I really appreciated this man's concern for my safety and well-being late at night, and thanked him profusely. It seemed like with each step of my solo journey to India, God provided someone to accompany me when I would rather not have been alone. Perhaps God sent angels?! Hebrews 13:1-2 says, "*Let brotherly love continue. Do not neglect to show hospitality to strangers, for thereby, some have entertained angels unawares.*" Apparently angels do roam the earth, and while I did not show hospitality to this man, I did show friendship and appreciation to him, and he showed concern and protection to me.

- ▌ Do you believe in angels/spiritual beings? _____
- ▌ Do you believe you have ever been protected by something supernatural? _____ If yes, please share your story if you are comfortable.

Wanting to experience the sights and sounds of this loud and hectic city of Calcutta, I decided to walk the streets again and get a close and personal look at the dire poverty for myself, and to look into the faces and eyes of the people who lived in this slum.  The world is a very small place for those who live there, since many never leave this city.  As I wound my way through the narrow, crowded, dirty streets, they all looked the same to me: one shop after another, meat hanging with flies swarming around it, little statues of the Hindu's many gods, clothes piled up waiting to be sold, etc.  Just like the rickshaw ride to my hotel, I knew I was once again lost, which happened so very easily in Calcutta. There were no large buildings or landmarks to assist me in figuring out where I was going or even in which direction I was walking.  I prayed, asked God to direct me and to keep me safe, and felt I may have acted foolishly by wandering the streets alone, unsure of where I was going.  I was completely trusting in God at this time, and realized more than ever that I needed a close, trusting, and loving relationship with Him, not just at this time, but always.

- ▌ Can you think of a frightening experience in your life where you knew you needed to trust God fully? _____
- ▌ Would you like to share that experience, and say how you felt? _____
- ▌ Once you are out of a desperate or frightening experience, do you have a tendency to forget about God? _____
- ▌ If so, why do you think that is the case? _____

_____

_____

Back home in Kentucky, I met another hospice patient who loved and trusted God completely, and who I enjoyed visiting very much; her name was Rose.  Rose was an elderly woman who was a wonderful, tender lady of God and had been a Christian for over sixty years.  Rose told me she appreciated her chaplain visits each week.  She said she loved having someone to talk to about the Lord, who was also excited about how the Lord works in our lives, and who was genuinely interested in hearing her stories and thoughts about the Lord (which I was).  She also enjoyed praying with me which I did with each visit. Rose was a delightful person.

■  Do you know anyone who is a truly delightful and loving person who you
    enjoy visiting? _____

■  What makes this person special to you?_____

    _____

(What characteristics do they have that you appreciate?)

■  Do you have those special characteristics, or do you wish you did?  _____

    _____

■  How do we obtain positive characteristics? _____

    _____

    _____

Rose lived in a comfortable home with her husband of sixty years, and
their son Tom often stayed with his parents to help out, despite the fact that he
had a home and a wonderful family of his own.  Tom was a warm and funny
Christian man, who, with tears in his eyes, often spoke tenderly and lovingly
about his mother.  Tom sometimes sat in the bedroom with her and me and
spoke about what a wonderful example his mother was of a fine, strong Christian
woman who everyone loved.  Cards, photos, flowers, and gifts in her room
displayed the love and affection people had for Rose.  Her warmth, tenderness,
and love were apparent, even as she lay dying with an oxygen mask on, often
struggling to breathe.  Rose could not get out of bed, so her family planted a
beautiful flower garden outside of her widow and hung bird-feeders so she could
watch the birds come and go.  Wind chimes sang in the breeze while the birds
seemed to almost dance to their melody.

■  Are there kind and simple things we can do for other people that we
    sometimes neglect? _____

    _____

■  How easy (or difficult) is it to look for ways to be kind and helpful to
    others? _____

    _____

On one of my visits, Rose spoke about her approaching death, and admitted that at times she was a little afraid. I asked her why she was afraid since she knew Jesus and was assured of her salvation. She looked straight into my eyes, with tears in hers, and said, "I am so sinful, and I know Jesus forgives me, but I wonder what I will feel like when I see Him. We all fall so far short." Rose knew she would soon be face to face with God, and began to really understand the holiness of God. Rose was a strong woman of God who had done many beautiful things for people all of her life.

- Is being a good person enough to get you into Heaven? _____
- Could Rose get to Heaven on her many good works? _____
- Do you know anyone who shows an unusual love and trust in God, and who obeys Him in all circumstances? _____
- Do you have a relationship with God?_____
- Do you trust God in all circumstances?_____

*"Jesus said to him, I am the way, the truth, and the life.*
*No one comes to the Father except through me."*

(John 14:6)

# Step Eleven:

## Understand Safety As Found In Scripture And In The Center Of God's Will

The promises of God, as they are found in the Bible, do not at all imply that those who are Christians and follow God's Word will at all times have an easy life, filled with all kinds of blessings, and that people who ignore God and His Word will have lives of pain. Jesus said that His Father in Heaven "*makes his sun rise on the evil and on the good, and sends rain on the just and on the unjust*" (Matthew 5:45). We are to live our lives according to God's Word because it makes sense, because God loves us deeply, and because He gives us a blueprint for successful, loving, and peaceful lives. The Bible gives us the tools that guide us and keep us safe.

If you have ever worked with tools, you know what a difference they can make in your work. When I first began painting as an apprentice painter, I went to trade school and was very poor. The contractor who hired me told me I had to bring a few of my own tools, including a latex brush. I had no idea what to buy, and with very little money, I went to a hardware store and bought a latex brush. I went to work, and really struggled trying to paint; I assumed it was because I was just learning, and part of it was that fact. However, during our work day, my boss came in and asked for a paintbrush, so I gave him mine. He painted for a few minutes, then threw the brush across the floor and said, "What is this thing! I can't paint with this!" After working for over twenty years as a painter myself, if someone gave me a cheap, non-professional paintbrush, I too would struggle and could not paint well either. The tools make all the difference. The paint just seems to flow with a good brush, while painting is really a struggle with a bad/ cheap brush.

The Bible is our "tool" or blueprint as well; following it can make your life flow and make sense, while disregarding it can make your life cheap and a real struggle.  Aside from God, what is the real meaning or purpose of life?  Disregarding the basic principles of Scripture and following our own often destructive paths can lead to chaos.  Staying stuck in any kind of addiction can make life a living hell.  Proverbs 26:11 says, *"Like a dog that returns to his vomit is a fool who repeats his folly."* Thinking you can do the same thing over and over and expect different results is the old saying for insanity or foolishness.  Many of us caught in addictions or sinful, harmful life-styles are like that dog returning to its vomit; it's not pretty.

- How many of you think, or have thought: "That will never happen to me.  I won't get addicted," or "I'll never overdose"? _____
- "I don't have a problem with this (fill in the blank); it's just fun"… but then it takes over your life. _____
- Have you ever felt like a dog returning to his vomit?_____

The founder of Veggie Tales (an animated children's series), Phil Vischer, was once asked in a board meeting where he wanted his new ministry to be in five years.  The board members were all anticipating some insightful business projections, visions, and future plans, but they heard something instead that surprised them.  Vischer's response was simple.  He said, "I want to be in the center of God's will." The founder of Veggie Tales said he begins each day in prayer and reading his Bible, which will keep him in that center.  We can only be in the center of God's will when we live according to Scripture and move in the right direction.  When we are in the place of surrender, obedience, and love, we can begin to recover who we really are, who we were created to be, and we can return to ourselves.

- How hard is it to surrender our wills? _____

_____

- How do we know who we are and what we were created to be and do?

_____

■ Are you living out your true self, or the self you want to be?_____
■ Where do you find safety, if at all? _____

_____

Maude was another one of my beautiful hospice patients who relied heavily on Scripture to guide her life.  The directions I was given to get to her house did not appear correct, but indeed they were.  There was a little run-down shack up on a hill that my car could not ascend, so I parked at the bottom of the gravel driveway and walked up to the old house.  Dogs, cats, and chickens greeted me on my climb, and they appeared to be dying for love and attention.  A woman shouted down to me from the porch (that I was sure would collapse under her weight, though she seemed completely unaffected by the disrepair), and said, "You must be the hospice nurse?" "No" I said.  "I hope I don't disappoint you, but I'm the chaplain.  Can I come in?" We both laughed, as she showed me where the gate was to the house.  I gently opened the gate, which almost fell off as I opened it.  As I approached the house, I heard a tap on a window and saw an old woman sitting, looking out, and motioned for me to come in.  I walked around to the back of the house to a porch with a ceiling that was barely six feet high, and opened the old, broken-down door to the kitchen where Maude sat.  It was a warm June afternoon, but Maude sat in front of an open oven door with heat pouring out, wrapped in a blanket, wearing a flannel night shirt and pajama pants. She reached out for me to hug her, and cried, "Oh thank you Jesus for sending me this woman." I did not think she even knew who I was! "Get yourself a chair and sit with me" she said.  I went into the next room, got an old wooden chair, sat close to her and held her hand as she started to speak.  "I just want someone to hear me, to listen to my dreams, and to hear my stories." "That's what I'm here for," I said.

■ Have you ever felt like Maude: you simply wanted to tell your story and be heard? _____
■ What prevents us from really listening to one another? _____

_____

▌ Why do so many of us feel so lonely; like no one wants to hear our stories or listen to our dreams? _____

_____

▌ Do you still have dreams for your life? _____ What are they? (please share as you are comfortable) _____

_____

_____

_____

Maude said she was tired of all of the problems, the struggles, and the "sins" of the world, and as she came to the end of her life, she simply wanted to live according to the words and Truth of the Bible.  Maude said she was tired of the lack of love in the world, and the indifference people had towards God and living good lives.

▌ Do you share Maude's concerns, or are you indifferent towards God and living a good life? _____

▌ If you are indifferent towards the Bible or living the life God wants you to live, what is your driving passion in life? In other words, what is it that you live for? _____

_____

_____

*"When David's time to die drew near, he commanded Solomon his son, saying, 'I am about to go the way of all the earth.  Be strong, and show yourself a man, and keep the charge of the Lord your God, walking in His ways and keeping his statutes, His commandments, His rules, and His testimonies, as it is written in the Law of Moses, that you may prosper in all that you do and wherever you turn."*

(I Kings 2:1-3).

# Step Twelve:

## Recover Yourself Through Scripture

Few people have touched my soul like my hospice patient George. He was dying of cancer at a relatively young age, leaving behind a fifteen year old son who had lost his mother (George's wife) to cancer when he was only three years old. When George learned of his diagnosis, he made plans and arrangements for his son to be cared for by his grandmother, George's mom, and already began moving things into her home for this difficult transition. Despite all of these challenges, George was not bitter or angry, but grew to love Jesus more and more with each day, as he knowingly drew closer to his death.

- If you knew you were going to die and leave behind a young child who had already lost their other parent, would you be angry and/or bitter? __

  _____

- How would you feel about God in a situation like George's? _____

  _____

  _____

When I would visit George each week in the hospital, he was calm, even happy, and he shared the Gospel of Jesus Christ with everyone who came into his room: nurses, maintenance workers, doctors, friends, and family. George would often give me a list of names for me to bring to my church to pray for, since he said they were people he knew who were not saved, and he wanted to see them in Heaven with him. Despite the fact that he was dying, George was one of the most thoughtful and considerate people I knew.

- How easy/hard would it be to think of others while you are dying, instead of focusing on yourself and your own situation? _____

  _____

▌ What allows someone to think of others before themselves, not just when they are in crisis, but on a daily basis? _____

_____

_____

On one of my visits, I told George that I was taking a short – term mission trip to India, so he gave me a book he wanted me to read on the plane (*A Hole in the Gospel,* by Richard Stearns, which I highly recommend). George was always thinking of the needs of other people. George had recently led a friend to the Lord from his hospital bed, which brought him great joy. When I told George how much I respected him for his heart and love for people, he said, "Well I know works won't get me into Heaven, only Jesus will, but I have a lot of missed time to make up for." George had a lot of regrets in life, including being involved in a murder many years ago for which he was never caught.

▌ Do you live with regrets for past actions in your life? _____
▌ Can you find peace and forgiveness from your past, believing God really does forgive all sins, including murder? _____

George was growing very weak, and he wanted to read the Bible, but did not have the strength to hold it. His eyesight was also growing dim, so his family bought him the Bible on CD, which he listened to for a large part of each day. George immersed himself in Scripture, and found a new sense of peace and security, as he laid in his hospital bed dying. The day before George died, I walked into his room; he looked at me, closed his eyes, and said, "Donna, it's just about that time." I asked George if he was scared, and he said he was not. I then asked if he felt God's peace, and he simply said with a smile, "I'm tired and ready." I stayed with George a little while longer and left so he could rest. George asked if I would see him the following day, and I told him I would try. God is good. I was supposed to go to a meeting that next day almost an hour away from the hospital, and there were several other patients I needed to see in that direction, but the meeting was abruptly changed to a location right across the street from the hospital where George was staying. After the meeting,

I stopped in to see George, and he looked bad.  George was having difficulty breathing due to an accumulation of fluid, and said he felt like he was smothering and could not catch his breath.  He began to panic and started reciting Psalm 23.  "Say it with me!" George said, as he grabbed my arm.  Together, we recited this beautiful Psalm, as I hit the nurses' call button.  I then held George's hand and we prayed together.  Within minutes, a nurse came into the room, and after I told her George's complaints, she administered some medication that allowed him to relax and breathe much easier.  I felt George's hand relax in mine, and then asked him if he wanted me to read some Scripture.  George nodded his head and smiled, as he was growing too weak to talk.  I read page after page to him, watching his smile grow with each word.  George wanted to hear the Word of God as he left the earth and entered into God's holy presence.  George fell asleep as I read, and woke up in Heaven, face to face with Jesus.  While literally dying, George knew the power of the Bible and of Jesus' love, mercy, and forgiveness.  George knew God reveals Himself and His love through Scripture, and he quietly left this earth to its powerful words.  George had recovered himself through Scripture because of its power to change hearts, minds and lives.

▋ Do you think the words of a book, such as the Bible, can change people?

_____

▋ How are words able to change hearts and minds? _____

_____

_____

▋ How is the Bible different from any other book? _____

_____

_____

▋ Do you think God and His Word can change your life like it did for George? _____

The stories I have recounted of my experiences in India and of my hospice patients display God's love, grace, mercy, and desire for all of us to find recovery through Him.  Through His Word, God places a path before us for a peaceful and orderly life, but many have chosen to ignore His blueprint and guide, and found lives that have not went in good directions.  God's love is so relentless, that no matter what our circumstances, He still speaks to us and affirms His love for us.  Unfortunately, some of us live our entire lives in chaos and confusion, never finding true peace, and miss out on God's rich blessings.  Living a life where God is first, and reading His Word to begin to understand who He is and what He wants for us, will not always be easy, but it will bring peace and blessings.  We all can truly find our recovery through Jesus and become the people were we meant to be.

*"All Scripture is inspired by God and is profitable for teaching, for rebuking, for correcting, for training in righteousness, so that the man of God may be complete, equipped for every good work."*

(II Timothy 3:16-17)

# Journey's End – Or Beginning?

*"Truly, truly, I say to you, unless a grain of wheat falls into the earth and dies, it remains alone; but if it dies, it bears much fruit. Whoever loves his life loses it, and whoever hates his life in this world will keep it for eternal life. If anyone serves me, he must follow me; and where I am, there will my servant be also. If anyone serves me, the Father will honor him"* (John 12:24-26).

Jesus spoke these words shortly before He was betrayed by His friends, tortured, and put to death on a cross. Jesus said that those who serve Him must follow Him and will be where He is. But Jesus knew He was about to die! What was He talking about? Jesus also mentioned that a grain of wheat has to die in order to bear fruit; so too, we must die to ourselves, to our selfish ways of life and our destructive habits in order to be like Him and receive honor from His Father. "Hating" our lives simply means we get sick of the things that hold us back from who we are meant to be, like the struggles, the sins, the bad habits, and the addictions that we have allowed into our lives, and basically kill them, so we can have new lives. Are you ready to do that?

Some churches teach that once we become Christians, our lives are always easy and good, that we will be happy and we will not struggle anymore, but that is not what Jesus taught. He actually said, "*In this world you will have tribulation. But take heart; I have overcome the world*" (John 16:33). God promises to stay with us, to help us, to give us the strength we need to overcome our individual problems, and to always love us. The Bible is not some magical book that makes all of our problems go away, but it is an important blueprint for our lives that will guide us, keep us on track, help us get through our lives in peace, and make sense of our world. The wisdom and guidelines in the Bible can also keep us from our self-inflicted problems, and most importantly, it can show us the very nature and character of God, and help us to live our lives in a manner pleasing to Him. When we please God, we will also find peace.

Many people put God in a box of their own limited minds, and make Him whoever they want Him to be, rather than discover who He really is. The Bible teaches us who God is, what He is like, what He expects from us, and how He can make us into the people that we actually long to be, but probably are not. God loves us no matter what we have done and no matter how we live, but He does not want us to remain in the muck and mire we so often live in; He has so much better for us!

Some of you may need to recover from alcoholism or drug addiction; some of you may not have those struggles, but we all struggle with something. We may all need to recover from the gods of our own making, or serving the god of our selfishness which led us down so many wrong roads. Recovery is found through an intimate relationship with Jesus Christ, who can be known through Scripture, which is our Blueprint for life. Prayer and fellowship with other believers will help us down our path and keep us on track. The Old Testament book of Judges describes people who do not want to recover from their sinful and foolish ways, and says, "*In those days there was no king in Israel; all the people did what was right in their own eyes*" (Judges 21:25). Their lives and their community were in chaos, and they were too blind to see. We need to end the chaos in our lives and learn a better way. Jesus Christ shows us a better way, and shows us how to be the person He wants us to be, and the person we want to be as well.

Let me leave you with the insightful and beautiful words of the late theologian Dietrich Bonhoeffer, who summed up what I hope you have learned in this study:

"*Man's apostasy from Christ is at the same time his apostasy from his own essential nature*" (Bonhoeffer, 110).

▌ What does Bonhoeffer's quote mean? _____
_____

_____

▌ Are you ready to recover yourself and find your own "essential nature?"

_____

_____

"The call of happiness is a call to the deep joy in life
that is found when one discovers one's place, purpose,
and identity in relationship with God."

(Benner, p. 116)

**"Peace to you brothers, and love with faith,
from God the Father and the Lord Jesus Christ.
Grace be with all who love our Lord Jesus Christ
with love incorruptible."**

(Ephesians 6:23)

# The Twelve Steps

1.  Admit that at times, we all pretend and are hypocritical.
2.  Acknowledge that we are lost.
3.  Discover God through Jesus Christ.
4.  Begin to develop a Christ-centered world view.
5.  Learn to see God in daily life.
6.  Deny yourself for the sake of loving others.
7.  Allow Jesus to be more, and yourself to be less.
8.  Learn to love, help, and live selflessly.
9.  Understand your will as it conflicts with God's will.
10. Learn to trust, love, and obey God completely.
11. Understand safety as found in Scripture and in the center of God's will.
12. Recover yourself through Scripture.

# References

*Alcoholics Anonymous, Fourth Edition.* Alcoholics Anonymous World Services, Inc. New York: 2001.

Anderson, Neil T. *Who I Am in Christ.* Bethany House Publishers, Bloomington, MN: 2001. (p 10&11)

Benner, David G. *Care of Souls: Revisioning Christian Nurture and Counse,* Baker Books, Grand Rapids, MI: 1998.

Bonhoeffer, Dietrich. *Ethics.* Collier Books, Macmillan Publishing Company, New York: 1963.

C.S. Lewis. *Christian Behavior.* The MacMillan Company, New York: 1945.

C.S. Lewis. *Reflections on the Psalms.* Harcourt Brace Jovanovich, New York: 1958.

The Holy Bible English Standard Version. Crossway, Wheaton, IL: 2008.

Kasik, Donna. *Recovery: A Return to the Self.* GreenWine Family Books, a division of GlobalEdAdvance Press, TN: 2010.

Lehe, Robert T. *God, Science, and Religious Diversity.* Cascade Books, Eugene, Oregon: 2018.

Mother Teresa. *No Greater Love.* New World Library, Novato, CA: 1989.

Oates, Wayne, editor and translator, *Basic Writings of Saint Augustine.* Baker Publishing, Grand Rapids, MI. 1980.

Poplin, Mary. *Finding Calcutta: What Mother Teresa Taught Me About Meaningful Work and Service.* Intervarsity Press, Downers Grove, IL: 2008.

Twelve Steps and Twelve Traditions. Alcoholics Anonymous World Services, Inc. New York: 2008.

# JOURNEY TO RECOVERY
## A Return To The Self

# About the Author

**Donna Junker** (née Kasik) has a Bachelor of Arts in Philosophy from North Central College in Naperville, IL, a Master of Divinity from Northern Baptist Theological Seminary in Lombard, IL., certification in Thanatology, certification in Christian Drug and Alcohol Counseling, as well as one year of Clinical Pastoral Education. She is an ordained chaplain through the World Council of Independent Christian Churches, and has six years experience working as the chaplain of a Rescue Mission, as well as many years working as a hospital and hospice chaplain.

Chaplain Junker's passion is cultural studies and mission work. She taught short-term intensives for six years at a seminary in Kenya, East Africa, ministered at Mother Teresa's home for the dying in Calcutta, India, and worked at an AIDS hospice in Zambia, Southern Africa.

Donna served in the Ministerial Association, and is active in her community and local church. A mother and doting grandmother, Donna lives in Kentucky with her husband, Dr. Paul Junker.

Books may be ordered at

www.gea-books.com/bookstore

or from the author

donnajunker@roadrunner.com

or any place good books are sold.

*The first four books were published under the author's maiden name: Donna Kasik.

# Books by the Author

**\*Three Weeks in Africa**
**ISBN: 978-1-935434-13-9**

"We as the American hospices are not sent to help the poor African hospices, but to deepen relationships with them, to assess needs and to discover how they function. We can share our knowledge with them, and they in turn can share their knowledge and insight with us." Hospice and Palliative Care is a new concept in Africa, and is established, funded and carried out in different ways than American hospices. The author's 3-pronged purpose in writing this book is to: 1) Approach hospice care from a missional point of view, 2) Share the importance of compassionate, faith-based end-of-life care, and 3) Understand and appreciate Zambia's challenges of hospice and palliative care.

**\*Kenya: A Priority on My Bucket List**
**ISBN: 978-1-935434-63-4**

A list of things to do or accomplish before exiting this life is called a bucket list. One of the items on the author's bucket list was to go somewhere in Africa to see the wild animals in their natural habitat. Little did she know that Kenya, East Africa would become like a second home and would offer far more than a safari ride. Traveling to Kenya seven times, the author gives a detailed account of her experiences and brings to light the clash of cultures which can cause misunderstandings between missionaries and Kenyans. The cross-cultural lessons learned in this book can be applied to missions anywhere.

## *Recovery: A Return to the Self
### ISBN: 978-1-935434-51-1

Using real-life situations, the author demonstrates principles and practices to recover the true self lost along the way. The blueprint the author used in her own recovery is like a roadmap to protect and guide - not just a rule book. As a hospice chaplain, the author witnessed first-hand the wisdom of the dying, but it was after working with the poor and dying in India that she created the spiritual 12-step program outlined in this book.

## *Thinking Outside the Box ...About Love
### ISBN: 978-1-935434-00-5

It begins with seeking and ends with discovery; it is a deeply personal story of warm hopes and cold realities. It is a journey of conviction, compelling both the writer and the reader to look at the world differently and start, Thinking Outside the Box.. About Love.  This book tells of Donna in the role of VA Chaplain who demonstrates true, Christian love for the lost and suffering.

## First Day Devotions
### ISBN 978-1-935434-87-0

In my work as a Chaplain/Pastoral Care Coordinator at the Lexington Rescue Mission in Lexington, Kentucky, part of my job is to write a weekly devotional for the staff. Each Wednesday afternoon I sit in my office, pray, and write my devotion, then email it to all of the staff. Each week several of the Mission staff sends me wonderfully kind and uplifting feedback from my devotions, which I do not deserve, but give glory to God if the devotionals have touched hearts and minds. After doing this part of my job for a couple of months, I decided to compile these devotions into a small book that could be used not only for the staff, but also for clients, and perhaps in homes and churches. I have included many of the devotions written at the Mission in this book and pray God uses them to uplift you.

**Meditations: A Collection of Weekly & Holiday Reflections**
**ISBN 978-1-434535-94-8**

As I wrote this book, my prayer was that the reader would not settle for a short devotion each week, with Scripture verses inserted into my thoughts, but that they would take some time every day, to read the words that bring healing, hope and life, which are found in the Word of God – the Holy Bible. If we stake our entire lives and eternity on our Christian faith, we must certainly know what that Faith teaches.

**Journey to Recovery: A Return to the Self**
**ISBN: 978-1-950839-15-5**

Recovery is not limited to addictions. Not all people suffer from addictions, but we all suffer from not always living as the people we want to be. Journey to recovery and a return to the self simply involve recovering the person who God created us to be, who many of us have lost along life's journey for many reasons, such as: abandonment, betrayal, pain, addictions, loss, etc. God has a plan for all of our lives and, no matter what the circumstances were surrounding our births, God created each of us as a unique person who He wants in this life. We are all valuable to God, and He wants us to live up to our full potential.